THE ISSUE WITH ALL CHURCH LEADERSHIP

Here's Why Your Church Rejected
YOU!

MARCUS L. BOSTON

TAMPA FLORIDA

MARCUS L. BOSTON

© 2023 Marcus L. Boston. All Rights reserved.

This book or part thereof may not be reproduced in any form, stored in a retrieval system or transmitted in any form by any means – electronic, mechanical, photocopy, recording or otherwise, without prior written permission by Marcus L. Boston except as provided by United States of America copyright law.

ISBN: 9781959275329

LIBRARY OF CONGRESS: 2023947191

| Dedication |

I dedicated this book to everyone rejected and mistreated by church leadership. Whether it was your pastor, his wife, the associate pastors or their wives, the ministers or their wives, the prophets and their wives, single ministers, deacons, bishops, the mothers of the church, the greeters, the ushers, dance leader, church staff, anyone who has a position in the church, or any combination of church leaders and their children. Be encouraged. God saw your tears. God understands your anger. Your prayers were heard. The answers are here. Be restored and made whole in Christ.

| Table Of Contents |

| Dedication | page 7

| Introduction | page 9

| Chapter One |
When You Joined The Church

———   page 12

| Chapter Two |
Your Growth In Christ

———   page 48

| Chapter Three |
Maturity in Christ

———   page 87

ABOUT THE AUTHOR
BOOKING INFORMATION
BOOKSTORE

| Introduction |

This book is an assignment. I was taking a shower when the Lord told me to write this book. Every church I've been a member of is guilty of what I'm going to write. I will share as many examples as the Lord desires from my own life and from the lives of others who also experienced this. This book is not an attack on the church, but this book will be a wake-up call to church leadership globally. I have yet to know of a church who isn't guilty of what's inside these pages. I will not be using any real names or describe anyone. I've been a Christian for 30 years, as of August 2023, and the member of 7 churches in 2 different states. This book is number 18. I've experienced many negative things in the church, but God has proven Himself to me many times. The purpose of this book is to restore the backsliders who left their church, and God, because of church leadership. For all church leaders who are guilty, repent, and change. Yield it to God in prayer and get deliverance. If you're mad or angry about this book I honestly don't care. If you're mad or angry, you are mad and angry at the Lord. This books second purpose is to purify the hearts of church leadership. Our hearts must be purified. Only the pure at heart shall see God. If any of us die and our hearts are not pure we will not spend eternity with Jesus. I pray for those who are hurting to be healed and made whole as they read. I'm very sure your answers are here. Come back to Christ and understand God wasn't the one who hurt you.

God bless you,

Marcus L. Boston author

| Chapter One |
When You Joined The Church

Chances are when you joined the church you also gave your life to Christ for the first time. What a joyous occasion. All of heaven is rejoicing with you because you gave your life to Christ. Jesus is very pleased you came unto Him. The cross was for you and for everyone who comes to Him. You are now a new creature in Christ and you are now born of the Spirit. You were baptized and you're excited about your new life in Jesus. If you didn't grow up in the church like myself, you are completely clueless about the church world. I gave my life to Jesus at the age of 22 in 1993. I believed everyone in the church were genuine good people. There was no internet and or smartphones. No online tools to help my Christian walk. I had no bible foundation. I couldn't quote a single verse. In the church I first joined I felt so much love. It's like the building was full of love radiating throughout the atmosphere. All the smiling faces and hugs made me feel so welcomed. I didn't understand most messages that came across the pulpit, but I enjoyed being around the people of God. I was no longer just Marcus. I was now Brother Marcus. It took some getting used to, but I embraced it. I embraced being Brother Marcus. I'm sure you did too. You were now a Brother or Sister in Christ. You were even more fortunate than this if you were called a son or daughter by your spiritual father or spiritual mother. Maybe you had both. You didn't just have a pastor in your life. You now have a spiritual father and his wife is your spiritual mother. This wasn't my case in my first church, but I know many people who's experience is exactly just like this. Nonetheless, we received Christ and that's the most important decision we've every made. The enemy hates this decision. The devil doesn't desire any of us to be with Jesus for eternity. Jesus said, "Hereafter I will not talk much with you: for the prince of this world cometh, and hath nothing in me." Jesus was and still is completely pure. There was nothing in Jesus the devil could use. Ephesians chapter 4 verse 27 says, "Neither give place to the devil." I mentioned in the introduction that we must all have pure hearts. If our hearts are pure the devil doesn't have anything he can use within us. If your heart isn't pure before the Lord those things within your heart can be used by the devil. We are not to give place to the devil or have any impurity in our hearts the devil can use. If your heart isn't pure you will know whether it is or isn't by the time you finish reading this book.

As you continued going to this church you eventually opened up and started fellowshipping, hanging out, and kickin' it with your church family. Yes, the body of Christ is your family now. We are taught to come out from among them and be ye separate says the Lord. Touch not the unclean thing. We have come out of darkness into the marvelous light. I was taught to stay away from, no, I was taught to cut off all friends who weren't saved. It's in this place of fun and laughs with my church family where it all started to unravel. I can't speak for you, but as for me, as I fellowshipped with them is where all the love began to change.

Now that I was a Christian and old things are now passed away, I talked about the old things I used to do. They weren't very far from me, but I stopped many things. I stopped going to the club and I fought like crazy not to fornicate. Oh by the way, I didn't know pre-marital sex was a sin. I had a girlfriend when I got saved and we were sexually active. You can read exactly how I became a Christian in my very transparent book, "A Pastor's Mistake. A Transparent Novel Testimony," and in my completely transparent book, "From Woman To Woman." Reader Discretion Is Advised. Let's continue. As I opened up sharing my life to my church family, I noticed my church family started changing. I thought it was me at first because I was a babe in the Lord. Since I was fresh out of the world my perception had worldly reactions. I was brutally honest. I didn't have Christian character yet. I was in the pastor's office every week for a season for something I said to someone in my church family. I was rebuked and corrected every time. Here's what I didn't write in my other books. When I brought situations to our pastor about my church family, well, they weren't getting rebuked about it. I was always told there was nothing wrong with what they said. It's amazing how God brings all things back to my remembrance as needed to write in books. I spent plenty of time with my church family and because I didn't know the bible at all, I didn't fully know when I was being treated wrong biblically. I'll provide verses soon.

If I have an accusation against someone at my church, it should be heard without interruptions. I should be given the time to explain myself until my heart is clear. I was interrupted and never given the chance to finish explaining myself. This is wrong pastors and church leadership. So what does the bible say about situations like this? My heart goes out to babes and new Christians. Especially when they don't know the bible at all. When you church leaders finesse new Christians, at some point those street smarts enter into play. At first when these things happen, new Christians and young Christians do not want to believe the situation. They tend to blame themselves until the day comes when it's completely clear they are being mishandled. I know because I did this so many times because I was from the world. This person has been in the church all these years so they must be right. To all of you new Christians, babes in the Lord, and all of you backslidden Christians, the people in the church can sin, they can mess up, and they can handle situations wrong. Pastors and church leadership are not perfect and they do not do everything right. There are many scriptures teaching them on how to handle the flock of God. God wants His sons and daughters in church leadership to deal righteously with everyone in the House of God. I love what Apostle Paul says in First Corinthias Chapter 13.

Read the entire chapter and return to this book.

Apostle Paul is saying clearly that love is more important than all of the manifested qualities in the body of Christ. Paul specifically called out all knowledge, all mysteries, speaking with the tongues of men and angels, having all faith, the gift of prophecy, and helping the poor. He said love is greater than all of these things and he said if he doesn't have love he is nothing. Apostle Paul is my example of what all church leadership should follow. There is no minister, pastor, apostle, or prophet today who is greater than Apostle Paul. We are the fruit of his ministry. Paul said he is nothing without love.

Church leadership, is your love perfect towards God's people? I'm sure you're going to say, "Yes." This is why Apostle Paul is my example for all people in church leadership. Paul took the time to explain love and used himself as an example. These verses are in the bible because church leaders needed to know this information. Jesus said in John chapter 13 verses 34 & 35, " A new commandment I give unto you, That ye love one another; as I have loved you, that ye also love one another. By this shall all men know that ye are my disciples, if ye have love one to another." Our love one for another would show everyone that Jesus is real. Isn't this amazing? If we as Christians love each other everyone would know for sure that we are disciples of Jesus. This verse is not centered only for the church leadership loving other positions in church leadership. First John chapter 3 verse 14, "We know that we have passed from death unto life, because we love the brethren. He that loveth not his brother abideth in death." The first church didn't play with love. This was serious business. If you don't love your fellow Christian sisters and brothers you abide in death. What does this mean? Only the pure at heart are going to see God. What's in your heart that's preventing you from loving your fellow Christians? Or maybe it's just one person who you just don't care for strongly. Jesus also said to love our enemies. I admit I do not like hearing many things that new Christians said they are guilty of, but always remember that Jesus died for those same sins. Don't end up being like the Pharisees and Sadducees. They were very critical in judgment. You need to be full of the love Christ. This generation has hookup culture, private snapchat, only fans, threesomes, hot girl summer, 304 phases, and more. Even if you find these things disgusting and distasteful, you still need to love the souls of these people. Church Leadership: how would you minister to a porn star? How would you minister to strippers? Drug dealers? Murderers? Felons? Child Molesters? Sex Traffickers? When they come to Jesus and join your church, are you going to love them like Jesus? Jesus said to love each other as He loves us. When they give their life to Jesus they are now Christians. When they open up and share their life, can you handle it? Jesus can. Is your nose turned up or is your face contorted right now? You need to ask Jesus to give you the same grace He has for them. Love is patient and kind. How patient are you with God's people? How kind are you? Can you pray effectively for them without judgment? If you can't do this your heart is not pure. Who am I to write this book? Well, who are you to be in Church Leadership? You needed to be saved too. Are you puffed up and arrogant right now? Are you self-righteous? Luke chapter 18 verse 11 through 14, "The Pharisee stood and prayer thus with himself, God, I thank thee, that I am not as other men are, extortioners, unjust, adulterers, or even as this publican. I fast twice in the week, I give tithes of all that I possess. And the publican, standing afar off, would not lift up so much as his eyes unto heaven, but smote upon his breast, saying, God be merciful to me a sinner. I tell you, this man went down to his house justified rather than the other: for everyone that exalted himself shall be abased: and he that humbleth himself shall be exalted." The Pharisee pointed out the things they never did to try to make himself look better as a person, but the Pharisee was not sin free. Just because you are not guilty of things that are considered disgusting, nasty, or deplorable, doesn't make you a better Christian. You're still guilty of sin and you still needed Jesus for salvation. Humble yourself and ask God to purify your heart so your love will be pure toward all Christians. Here's how Jesus delt with Church Leadership in the bible.

Church leadership today has its flaws and so did the churches in the book of Revelation. In Revelation chapter 2 verse 1, the Lord is dealing with the angel of the church in Ephesus who is the person in charge; the pastor / church leadership. In verse 4 Jesus says this church has left their first love. In verse 5 they were required to repent because they were in a fallen state. They needed to do their first works again. This church needed to start over.

In verse 14 Jesus has issues with the church in Pergamos. This church has the doctrine of Balaam.

Balaam is found in Second Peter chapter 2 v. 15, Jude verse 11, Numbers chapter 22, and Numbers chapter 24. Balaam operated in witchcraft and performed enchantments for money. You can study Balaam and learn the full extent of everything he operated in. The spirit that used Balaam, which is identified by his name, is the same spirit that is now in the leadership of the church in Pergamos.

In verse 20 the Son of God says he has something against the leadership of the church of Thyatira. The church leadership allowed Jezebel to function in their church. Jezebel was King Ahab's wife in First Kings chapter 18 through Second Kings chapter 9. You're going to want to read it all straight through. Just like Balaam, the spirit that used Jezebel is identified by her name. The spirit of Jezebel was now functioning in this church and Jesus had a serious problem with the angel / pastor / church leadership of this church. The spirit of Jezebel has functions that can destroy a church.

In Revelation chapter 3 verse 2, Jesus said to the church in Sardis I have not found your works perfect before me. In verse 4 Jesus highlights there are a "few" names in Sardis which have not defiled their garments, and they shall walk with Him in white for they are worthy. How big was this church? We don't know. In the book of Acts chapter 1 verse 41 says 3000 souls got saved the day the Holy Ghost fell. Acts chapter 2 verse 47 says the Lord added to the church daily. Nonetheless, only a few of what every number were found faithful in this church and will walk with Jesus in white. Only a few!

In verse 15 Jesus has an issue with the angel of the church of Laodiceans. Jesus pointed out this church was neither hot nor cold. In verse 17 Jesus says this church is wretched, miserable, poor, blind, and naked. I'm not here to do a thorough study on these churches. I'm only highlighting Jesus dealing with the issues He had with His church leaders.

The church of Philadelphia in verses 7 through 13 didn't get rebuked or corrected. Jesus says in verse 8 he's given them an open door. They have a little strength. They kept His word and has never denied the name of Jesus. Then Jesus explained what He's going to do for them and how he is going to protect them from temptation in verse 10. Jesus blessed this church for their obedience and faithfulness to Him, and on the hand, Jesus warned several other churches of the consequences if they do not repent or turn from those things Jesus was against. Which brings us to today.

First Peter chapter 4 verse 8, "Above all, love each other deeply, because love covers over a multitude of sins." Love covers a multitude of sin. I understand why I experienced many things by the hand of church leadership. When I was a new and young Christian it hurt me deeply. I ended up backslidden behind church leadership. I didn't understand the grace of God. I didn't know I could come boldly before the throne of grace. I didn't know God was faithful and just to forgive me if I asked. Here's an excerpt from my first book in it's third edition, "A Pastor's Mistake."

"When Sunday arrived, I was very excited to be on my way to the House of God, although it was my former church. When I pulled up, no one was outside as I parked my car. Church had already started. As I stood at the door, I could not turn the doorknob to enter. I stood there for several minutes, holding the doorknob, as I thought about the reason I left this church in the first place. I fornicated with a sister who also attended this church. This is "Church Girl" in my tell-all book, "From Woman To Woman" Volume Two. When it happened, I didn't try to hide my sin. I went to our pastor, confessed my sin, and asked for prayer. Our pastor prayed for both of us in private at the same time. Moreover, I went to several of the ministers, told them what happened, and asked them for prayer. I felt so guilty and horrible for having sex with her. This act of fornication was devastating to me. I had been abstaining for almost three full years. I was looking forward to testifying when I reached the exact three-year mark, but it never happened. (A Pastor's Mistake paragraph 2 page 12)

"Finally, I turned the doorknob and entered my former church. All heads were on me and many mouths dropped in amazement at my presence. The service was already in progress and I actually felt good as I joined in the praise with the clapping of my hands. It was such a good feeling to be in the House of God once again. I looked around as I clapped my hands. A few saints gave me some ugly looks, but I also received a few smiles. My first service back was very nice and I had a great time. When church was over, I went and greeted everyone. I was so happy to see them again, in spite of the things that happened. Some were not happy at all to see me, but I really didn't care. I'm back on the Lord's side and that's all that mattered to me. Never again would I let anyone make me believe God doesn't love me. God brought me back to Himself without the assistance of anyone. He came into my residence to save me. There was no prophecy or someone laying hands on me. God Himself heard my cry and brought salvation to my soul. I will never walk away from God again because I now know that He is a forgiving God." (A Pastor's Mistake paragraph 1 page 22)

I am so grateful to God for restoring my soul in Christ. I left my church because I overheard the church leadership saying, I lost my salvation, God doesn't love me anymore, and God has departed from me. Can you imagine a young Chirstian hearing these words? Some of you heard these words before in some fashion. I know people who've overheard terrible things by their own pastor concerning their lives. That's probably why you're reading this book. If you're backslidden there's a scripture that says God is married to the backslider. "Turn, O backsliding children, saith the Lord; for I am married unto you:" Jeremiah chapter 3 verse 14. God is married to you. God never stopped loving you. It was your church leadership that didn't love you. Your church was wrong. Regardless of why it happened God loves you. God has not rejected you. I'm writing this to those of you who left your church and God because of how the church leadership mishandled you. I'm not talking to you people who backslid on your own. However, if you are backslidden, God loves you and never stopped loving you. God is married to you and desires you to come back to Him.

In my case, I left the church because of what they said which devastated me. The thought of God not loving me anymore had me suicidal. I had no children until I was backslidden. I was depressed and tormented with evil dreams. Here's how God brought me back to Himself.

"In the month of November 1998, while alone in my apartment, I cried out to the Lord to come save me from my sins. I had been in a backslidden condition for almost two years and was dreadfully missing the presence of the Lord. Several hours passed by, as I cried watching Fred Hammond's live concert on VHS; six hours to be exact. I kept rewinding and listening to the videotape, over and over repeatedly, as the tears flowed. Suddenly, I fell on my face sobbing and weeping as I felt the presence of God enter my living room. I realized immediately that the Lord heard my cry. While I was still on my face, my left hand started turning in a circular motion. I kept trying to stop my hand from turning, but to no avail. Then I heard the Lord say, "I'm wiping the slate clean." After the Lord had spoken those words, He began to purge me and afterwards, tears of appreciation began to fall rapidly. God was cleaning me and destroying those things that had me bound since I left the church in February 1997. God proved that He truly loved me and it felt so good to know that God heard me as I cried out for His hand of salvation." – A Pastor's Mistake paragraph 1 page 8

If God never came to get me Himself I would still be lost today. I hated every church everywhere because what I experienced at one church. When I returned to this church I apologized to those I talked about like a dog when I was backslidden. I repented for talking bad about all churches because of an experience at one church. My book "A Pastor's Mistake" is mostly about a pastor who misled me. He used prophecy to control me. I learned so much through these experiences and this is why they are written in books to help others who experienced the same thing. My second book, "Tainted Influence. Identifying Prophetic Truth & Error" teaches on everything good and bad about prophecy. You receive the total package pertaining to prophecy and the prophetic to avoid being misled or controlled by prophecy. Love would not control anyone in the House of God. God does not control us. No one should be controlled in any walk of life. If you need to get your pastor's permission to do anything, well, you are controlled. If you can't make a decision without first talking to your pastor, you are controlled. I'm not talking about having a consultation or asking for their opinion on a major decision. I mean you can't do anything at all without first talking to your pastor. Control is not love.

Now that I'm mature in the word of God, here's what should have happened when I approached the ministers of God saying I sinned. "Brethren, if a man be overtaken in a fault, ye which are spiritual, restore such a one in the spirit of meekness; considering thyself, lest thou also be tempted." Love would restore a person's soul to Christ. Love should cause a Christian to put themselves in the shoes of the person who sinned. Considering yourself shows you have compassion and demonstrate the love you desire to receive if you sinned. Love will not have you gossiping and spreading the sin of a brother or sister in Christ to other people. Love covers. Love does not expose, spread, share, and tell everyone about the sins and failures of individuals in Christ. Consider yourself. What if this was you? It's ok. That's why I'm writing this book and written other books to help the people of God hurt by no loving, no compassionate, and no grace of God filled Christians. Now that I think about it, this is probably why so many church leaders are being openly exposed and shamed online. They probably didn't show any love and grace when members of their church sinned. You judged and hurt them. They left your church broken and shattered. Just like I did. In my case I cried out to God not knowing this is a biblical thing to do. Psalm 77, Psalm 3 verse 4, Psalm 61 verse 1, Psalm 18 verse 6, and there are many, many, many more verses on crying out to God. Even now I can say this verse and say God did exactly what His words says. "O Lord my God, I cried unto thee, and thou hast healed me." Psalm 30 verse 2. I was clueless, but my heart, no, my spirit or the Holy Spirit knew what I didn't know. I truly had no bible knowledge. It took me awhile to understand the bible. As a matter of fact it took some years. I had layers of issues that I can identify now in my life in retrospect. Where was my pastor? What about looking for the lost sheep? My pastor never came to my residence looking for me. My pastor didn't call me either. This is sad. If you're in a mega church, ok I get it, but I was at churches who had things in place where certain people were in charge of checking on a certain number of members. Did your church have these things in place and no one called you? Did anyone look you up online? After the Lord brought me back to Himself, I was always the person looking for people who stopped coming to church. My heart ached for the babes and young Christians. They are victims too many times and it seemed like no one cared enough to come looking for them. If you're a person who looks for the saints who stopped coming to your church, good job. Someone has to do it. Its harder to do this at bigger churches unless they sit in the same section every week. Nonetheless, good job to the soul seekers and soul restorers. Amen. I cried out to God for 6 straight hours and He came to me Himself.

Romans 12 v 10, "Be kindly affection one to another with brotherly love; in honor preferring one another."

It would be nice if most church leadership would prefer the members of their church before themselves. Church leaderships are public servants right? Why do so many churches have church members serving the church leaders, but the church leadership is not serving their church members? What I just said is a conversation piece. I expect this to be a topic on podcasts and bible studies. "You have to serve before you can be elevated." "You can't just receive Christ and get on the platform. You have to serve first." I agree no babes should be elevated, and I do agree with all Christians serving in our churches, but why doesn't the church leadership serve their members? If you're full time ministry you should be doing a lot for your congregation. If you work a full time job you still have to find time for the flock of God. I don't want to hear your excuses why you can't. If you can't handle the position you have in church leadership then you need to resign. As we read our bibles and see exactly how our churches are supposed to be, we get discouraged. I know I've been discouraged seeing how the church acts and reading what the church should be doing. No church is perfect, but if the love in the church was perfect, I believe there would be better structures in church to minister to the congregation in love. Critical judgments when church members sin would not exist. I'm not talking about criminal sin. If you do something to go to jail, well, go to jail. Child molesters, rapists, thieves, etc., go to jail. Even the bible says suffer not as an evil doer. (First Peter chapter 4 verse 15.) Perfect your love church leaders.

Here's an example I wrote in my book "A Pastor's Mistake" of a family leaving a church because of church leadership.

"After Eddie and Carol were married, they never came back to our church again. I looked for them week after week, but they never came back. I was so hurt and missed them sincerely. I tried calling them, but their number was changed. At least I was a part of their special day and that meant a great deal to me. I really missed them." – A Pastor's Mistake page 175 (Someone gave me Eddie's new phone number and I called him.)

"When I heard Eddie's voice on the other end of the phone I was overjoyed. He and I talked for about an hour. I asked him why they left our church and he didn't waste any time sharing the reason why. He said, "On the day of our wedding, I overheard Pastor Davis talking with one of my groomsmen. Pastor Davis said he didn't like big weddings because they didn't work out most of the time. That crushed me on the inside Brother Marcus." Eddie felt as though Pastor Davis was saying his marriage wasn't going to work out. I tried to say that was probably just Pastor

Davis' opinion about big weddings, but Eddie cut me off, and put his wife on the phone. Now Carol had a straight tongue and she declared some things that truly caused me to be upset. She strongly expressed, "During our wedding reception, I overheard several leaders of Pastor Davis' church talking negatively about our wedding ceremony and the reception." Carol was very specific on who said what and how they said it. After hearing Carol speak her feelings, I knew she was telling me the truth. The comments she exclaimed these leaders made I heard them use those same words, and comments before about someone else, when I was in the inner circle. I understood why they were upset. They should have never overheard those things on their wedding day and those words should have never been spoken in the first place; especially openly where anyone could have overheard them. After I knew the reason why they left our church, I didn't try to get them to come back. I prayed for God to send them to another ministry where they could grow, and prosper in their walk with God. They also told me how they gave several people in our church money for using our church for their wedding. I was astonished at this information. No one else paid anything for the use of our church. The church was free for all members. They said they paid Pastor Davis, the Minister of Music, and a few others for their services with their wedding. I was really astonished and didn't want to believe what they told me. I really felt bad about the entire situation behind Eddie and his wife leaving our church, but there was nothing I could do about it." paragraph 2 page 211

Church leaders, are you guilty of doing anything like this? These things should never happen. Pure love would have never charged these members of the church money since no one else paid. Those words spoken by the pastor and other church leaders should have never been released. If you wanted to say these words, you should say them in secret unless you really wanted to be overheard. This is so sad. Church leadership work on perfecting the love of Christ. No one should ever hear their pastor or anyone in church leadership talking about them in any capacity. Why do this? Let me give you an example of what I experienced.

The character named "Remarkable" in my tell-all book, "From Woman To Woman Volume Three" shared what she and I did sexually to the people who were around us. My tell-all books are extremely transparent. Reader discretion is advised. 18+

readers only. These books contain my life before Jesus, how I received Jesus, and my life after Jesus. I wrote these books to show everyone about the outstanding grace of God the Lord delivered to me. You already read how I cried and God came to restore my soul in Him. I have many testimonies through my L's (Losses) and failures in Christ. Everyone needs the grace of God. The book covers for my tell-all series are racy on purpose. I talk about my failures, short comings, and sins freely because Jesus wanted me to. I didn't clean it up for readers either. I write books to edify. I do not write books to expose sin in the lives of people or to bring shame upon anyone. I use my life as an example to other Christians about the grace God has bestowed upon me. I detail my sins and personal issues in an effort to encourage other Christians to understand the love of Christ. I've overcome many things within the House of God by the people of God. I share these situations to encourage other believers to overcome as well. When my first book was released in 2007, I received plenty of hateful emails and messages online. Christians believed I was using real names and exposing people. We see this clearly today with various podcasts which use real names, pictures, and videos. This is not what

I'm doing. You just read earlier in the bible where Jesus called out the issues in His church. Why did He do this? Because He desires His people to get it right with Him. Why? So we all will go to heaven. This is why I write books to the body of Christ. I desire to see all of us make it in Christ. Everyone hurt by the church, I desire to see them healed and restored in the Lord. I desire every church to operate in the love of Christ and the grace of God.

Like I was saying about Remarkable, she told the people around us that we had sex. The people around us knew me well. I was abstaining from sexual sin and my life was clearly Christian. We attended the same church and when everyone suddenly knew we had sex I believed she was the one who told it. I thought she made phone calls and texts to people at our church. She and I had a talk some time in 2020. We shared our hearts and when she asked me if I still attended the church we both attended during our dating experience, I told her I no. I suppose we both stopped going to this church around the same time. I thought she still attended that church. As we talked I received a "word of knowledge." The Lord immediately informed me she wasn't the one who spread our information. I instantly knew who was the real guilty party. At this church I shared my heart with someone I trusted in the church leadership. There's a verse that says confess your faults one to another. I believed this church leader had a heart of love and compassion. Well, this church leader told all the other church leaders, and then they told others in our church, who told others in our church. It was one big mess. Here's the information I shared in my book, "BE CAREFUL WITH GOD'S DAUGHTER" paragraph 1 line 14 page 42, without mentioning what I'm about to say "now" in this book.

"Oh, she told those around us that we had sex. I am a man of God and this brought me great reproach. My name became mud. I was talked about very badly. Once our entire church knew we had sex, the entire atmosphere of our church was negative against me. As soon as I entered the sanctuary, I received a very bad headache every service and I had this headache during the entire time I was in the sanctuary. When I left the sanctuary the headache left me immediately. I was no longer free to praise and worship the Lord in my church. People in leadership stopped talking to me altogether. They walked passed me without speaking and talked to the person a few feet from me. I'm not exaggerating. This situation was so bad I resigned from my church simultaneously giving up the position I held in leadership. I didn't defend myself. Once the hearts of a church are against you, especially in the leadership, it's over. I moved on because I had to. There was no more grace to be at this church. I wasn't removed from my position by our pastor, maybe I beat him to it, but I was no longer respected."

The dynamics of this entire situation has changed and I'm free to talk about it. I only wish I wrote it originally in my book. I was so used to leaving this information out of a conversation. At one time I couldn't freely talk about it for obvious reasons. Well, the person in church leadership I trusted shared my sin with others in church leadership. I desired someone praying with me because many times when I have sinned sexually, I ended up being bound sexually for a season. Remarkable and I only had sex one time, and I wasn't trying to stay in sin. This is why I asked for prayer with someone I trusted. I was crushed by this person spreading my information. When I receive headaches in atmospheres it's typically informing me that lots of demons are present. In more critical situations it's demons, witchcraft, and curses in the atmosphere. For information on witchcraft get my books, "Enchanted. How Witches Attacked Me," and "Running Through The Darkness. The Story I Don't Want To Share." The atmosphere in our church was totally against me now. A person outside of our church leadership approached me saying, "Just stay focused on God. Don't worry about what anyone is saying." Well, I was focused on God and I could really careless what people are saying about me. However, when it's your church that's a different story. Church is called a sanctuary for a reason. A sanctuary is a "place of refuge," "a sacred place," and "the holiest part of a sacred place." When your church is against you it is no longer considered a place of refuge. I love praise and worship. I am faithful to God in corporate praise and worship. I could no longer open up at all in the sanctuary during praise and worship. How sacred is the church when your church is gossiping, slandering, and destroying your name? How holy is your church when everyone is judging you for your sins? No one tried to restore my soul. I didn't leave God or backslide. I prayed about going to a new church and moved on with my life. If you want to know what else happened with Remarkable please read my tell-all books.

Church leadership must always function in the love of Christ. When the church leadership operates in judgment you are now out of order biblically. Judgment doesn't cover sin. Judgment exposes sin. Judgment does not restore. Judgment does not have the grace of God. Judgment day will not have any grace. Hebrew chapter 9 verse 27, "And as it is appointed unto men once to die, but after this the judgment." When the church judges it's members without restoring their soul, you are discouraging. If it's a new Christian who doesn't know they can go boldly before the throne of grace, they will backslide because they weren't restored in love. I've seen this happen too many times through my 30 years as a Christian. Why do Christians act as if they have never sinned? Let me go further. Why do Christians act as if they don't sin anymore? Young Christians, new Christians, and unbelievers reading this book for information purposes only, everyone commits sin after receiving Jesus as their Lord and savior. If you seek the Lord your life will become better and the sins you're guilty of become less as you grow in the grace of God. Key word is "grow." I can safely say I'm not guilty of many things like I was 30 years ago. However, when I am guilty I know to repent and turn from it. I understand I should not practice sin or sin habitually. I know not to live in sin or let sin thrive in my life. After Christians get passed the sins we consider shameful, many do other things that are still sin. Gossip is sin. Read Ephesians chapter 4 verses 22 through 32. Please read it now. Verse 29 says let no corrupt communication proceed out of your mouth. <u>Corrupt</u> : to ruin morally. Tainted. Putrid. Depraved. To Spoil. To make rotten.

Gossip ruins a person's reputation. Gossip taints, spoils, and causes someone's name to be rotten. Most mature Christians know this and this is why it's just as bad as fornication, adultery, and homosexuality. Gossip is also known as "seeds of discord." (Proverbs chapter 6 verses 16 through 19) God hates seeds of discord. It's an abomination! Homosexuality is an abomination and so is seeds of discord.

Abomination: 1. a person or thing that is disgusting.
2. an action that is vicious, vile, etc.
3. intense loathing.

Gossip: a conversation involving malicious chatter or rumors about other people:

Gossip is not the love of Christ. Gossip exposes. Gossip uncovers. Although God hates seeds of discord, so many Christians continue to do it. Once again, only the pure at heart shall see God. What is in your heart causing you to gossip? What is in your heart helping you sow seeds of discord? You need to identify it and ask God to wash you, purify, and cleanse you of it.

I recall when I was infected with seeds of discord. In my case God corrected me. I heard information about a brother in Christ and when I saw him in church, I changed directions so I didn't have to talk to him. In that same moment I received a rebuke from the Holy Ghost that moved quickly up from my belly. Let me share how God speaks for a moment and then continue.

"In my prophetic classes I was taught three primary methods of how God uses us with prophecy. The first was through "<u>mental images or pictures</u>," the second was through "<u>physical sensations and heartfelt impressions</u>," and the third was through "<u>hearing words, or words in thought</u>." When I heard this information in class I nodded my head in agreement because of how God has used me in prophecy without this information. I didn't have this understanding or knowledge at that time, but I saw pictures when I was prophesying to people. Sometimes I had open eye visions that I called movies during that season. On both occasions I only spoke what I saw in the pictures and visions. Moreover, there were times when I felt a strong jolt that went through my body which started at my stomach. I now understand that it was physical sensations from the Holy Ghost. It seems to go through me as quickly as lightning flashes, and it feels like God uploaded what I needed to tell someone. On some occasions God used physical sensations to give me personal instructions. On a few occasions I've heard the voice of God. It took me many years to get to know God's voice, and sometimes today I ask God to give me three words of confirmation just to be sure. There were times when I thought I heard from God when I didn't and there were times when I didn't think it was God speaking to me and it was Him speaking. It is a learning experience reader, but I hope this information will benefit you." From my book "Tainted Influence. Identifying prophetic Truth & Error" Paragraph 2 line 2 page 38.

Like I was saying, God spoke to me through a physical sensation from Holy Ghost. It was instructions saying do not avoid your brother in Christ, turn around, and speak to him. Guess what? The talk we shared he needed it like we need to breathe oxygen. My heart wasn't pure anymore toward my brother, but God helped me press through the impurities in my heart that came from the gossip and seeds of discord I received about his sin. As I talked to him the Spirit of God came around us. God moved for both of us that day as we talked. As we talked God reminded me of what I went through with church leadership and let me see my brother was experiencing the same thing with church leadership. After I heard him I knew God's grace was with him and I learned to never act like this again. God purified my heart toward him and God encouraged him through me. Anytime something you heard causes you to change toward anyone, you heard and received seeds of discord. The unity and fellowship you once shared is now broken by what you heard and received. You now avoid them and stopped talking to them altogether. Where is the grace of God in these actions? Where is the love of Christ in these actions? I'm so glad the Lord rebuked me and instructed me on what to do.

"If we confess our sins, he is faithful and just to forgive us our sins, and to cleanse us from all unrighteousness." First John chapter 1 verse 9

"Let us therefore come boldly unto the throne of

grace, that we may obtain mercy, and find grace to help in the time of need." Hebrews chapter 4 verse 16

"For by grace are ye saved through faith; and that not of yourselves: it is the gift of God: Not of works, lest any man should boast." Ephesians chapter 2 verses 8 & 9

"For all have sinned, and come short of the glory of God; Being justified freely by his grace through the redemption that is in Christ Jesus." Romans chapter 3 verses 23 & 24

These verses are for the babes, new Christians, and backslidden Christians. Those who left their church because of the church leadership. I understand why you left. You just read my own person life information. I'll share more experiences from my personal life momentarily. Every church I've been a member of has church leadership who are guilty of this. In several of these churches the pastor was also guilty of doing or saying things that caused their church members to leave shattered and backslidden. To those who left God and their church, I humbly ask you to go boldly before the throne of God's grace. Repent unto God for leaving Him and come back to Him. After you give your life back to God, please let Him lead you and guide you. Like I said previously, there are no perfect churches, but know that God loves you whether or not the church leadership loves you.

"Let brotherly love continue."

Hebrews chapter 13 verse 1

"Faith works by love."

Galatians chapter 5 verse 6

Brotherly love should always be very prevalent in every church. Every church should be filled with love toward each other and toward those who visit your church. Isn't it amazing that "faith" works by love? This makes sense to me why many prayers seem to go unanswered. Could it be that the person praying really doesn't have love for the person they are praying for? Jesus said on a few occasions that he couldn't perform many miracles because of a lack of faith. Could it be that the churches that have documented miracles taking place on a regular basis actually have a heart full of love? We know Jesus loves us and he said greater works we shall do. Various times in the bible you read Jesus was with compassion and performed a miracle.

<u>Compassion</u>: a deep sympathy for the sorrows of others, with an urge to alleviate their pain.

If only we all as Christians were filled with compassion. If only our hearts were full of love toward each other. Jesus said love our enemies. Many of us do not love each other. How can we love our enemies if we can't really love each other? I'm challenging the church of the living God to love each other. I'm included. No one is excluded. If you die and leave this world without love toward everyone, do you think you're going to heaven? Heaven is a place that is prepared. It's already prepared. It's not getting any bigger. It's finished. It's a completely prepared place for those Christ knows will be with Him for eternity. On the other hand, hell is enlarging itself making room for more souls. (Isaiah chapter 5 verse 14) Who wants to stand before Jesus without a heart full of love for everyone? Only the pure at heart shall see God.

"Examine yourselves, whether ye be in the faith; prove your own selves. Know ye not your own selves, how that Jesus Christ is in you, except ye be reprobates?"

| Chapter Two |
Your Growth In Christ

Your growth in Christ is extremely important. I'm going to point out some things you need to do to grow in Christ and then we will continue about church leadership. "Wherefore laying aside all malice, and all guile, and hypocrisies, and envies, and all evil speakings, as newborn babes, desire the sincere milk of the word, that ye may grow thereby: if so be ye have tasted that the Lord is gracious." First Peter chapter 2 verses 2 & 3. When I first received Christ, I was surrounded by other new Christians and some mature Christians. I experienced many of these things you just read in First Peter. There were a lot of things that took place that had me in the pastor's office getting rebuked. It was always something I said that was brought to our pastor. However, when I brought things to our pastor, no one was rebuked or corrected. Even things that clearly upset me. There was a lot of confusion and fights that took place among us until I got to the point where I didn't hang around anyone from my church anymore. My biggest issue in this season was simple. I wasn't taught how to grow in Christ. There were no instructions on how to grow in Christ. I didn't understand the bible and I didn't know how to pray. Nowadays there are online tools to help any level of Christian grow. I didn't have this access in the 90s.

To grow in Christ you must desire the sincere milk of the word of God. However, Peter added, "if so be ye have tasted that the Lord is gracious." Taste also has a definition of, "Experience." When I gave my life to Christ I experienced Him. I didn't believe the bible at that time in my life. Here's how I became a Christian.

"The timeline in my life has now shifted. I gave my life to Jesus, and left Adorable alone. We were still friends. I was now trying to get my woman to go to church with me, but she refused to go. Therefore, I broke up with her. How did I become a Christian? Karen became a Christian and asked me to drop her off at a bible study. I agreed. I planned to go to a party that night that Karen was unaware of. When I dropped her off, she asked me if I wanted to come in. I declined. But, I heard a voice say "Go Inside." I started looking around and followed her into an apartment; not a church. When I entered this apartment, we were greeted by everyone.

There was a conversation that was taking place that immediately grabbed my attention. This woman was telling her dream to another woman. I was paying attention to every detail. I finally interrupted her and repeated the details of her dream that she had already shared. Then I began to ask did a, b, and c, happen next. She said it did. Then I asked if d, e, f, happen next and her eyes got so big. She almost yelled, "You're the guy in my dream!" I replied, "And you're the woman in my dream." Everyone was in awe at what just took place. This woman and I had the same dream of each other. This is the only time I've ever had a dream of anyone and met them, and learned that they had the same dream about me. This dream talk kept me longer than I planned on being there. The preacher was late, and as I got up to leave, he was walking in. He asked me to stay and I did. He preached some message on Adam and Eve. I personally didn't believe anything he just preached on. Remember, I don't believe the bible at this time. This preacher began talking to me and declared, "There's something you're looking for, and you're going to find it. You wanted to be at some party tonight, but God brought you here. (My eyes stretched wide because no one knew about the party I wanted to go to but me.) That wasn't a man in your closet when you were a little kid, that was a demon assigned to destroy your life. (My eyes stretched wider because that was the truth. I used to tell my mom there was a man in my closet and he's trying to get me.) You see what I'm doing, you're going to be doing it too." He said a lot more about my personal life that I won't add. That information might be in future books. Nonetheless, I looked at the bible someone let me use for that bible study and said in my thoughts, [This bible is for real!] No one at this bible study led me to Christ on this night. I went home and gave my life to Jesus alone, but I didn't know the bible, I didn't understand the bible, and only knew what the church taught me." From my book FROM WOMAN TO WOMAN page 186 paragraph 1 (My From Woman To Woman tell-series books are for 18+ readers only. Why did I write these books? I never did drugs, smoked, gangbanged, or went to prison. My sins were predominately sexual. Every man was not out in the streets in the same way.)

    I experienced Jesus through a minister who

operated in the spiritual gift "word of knowledge." Word of knowledge is the knowing of information supernaturally by the Holy Spirit / Holy Ghost. Word of knowledge is a gift from Jesus. This minister told me about my childhood and other things that I didn't openly talk about to my friends. I was looking for the truth about God. I was involved in the African Religion Yoruba prior to this night, and after learning everything about Yoruba, I asked the African Priestess this.

"I kept learning everything until I finally asked, "So, how do you get into this religion?" She detailed, "Well, you have to be initiated. You will have to shave your head. You will be given a tattoo of the symbol of the Orisha you will serve on your head. You'll be in a dark room for several days alone…" I interrupted her, "…Why would I be in a dark room several days alone?" I interrupted her again before she could explain why, "…So, let's say I get into this religion and then one day… I decide… I don't wanna be in it anymore. Can I just walk away?" "NO!" She practically shouted. "If you walk away the Orisha you dedicated your life to will kill you." On that note I became unsure of what to do and voiced, "Well, I need to think about this before I make a decision."

She understood.

This is the untold story of what happened before I prayed my last prayer which is in the Preface of "A Pastor's Mistake." I prayed "God, I believe you exist, but I just don't know how to get to you. I don't even know who to call you. I just don't believe all these religions lead to you. As of today, I am no longer looking for you. But if you give me the truth about you, I'll live it." I've heard too many ministers saying how they weren't even thinking about God while they were in sin, but I was; I was looking for Him. I even feel His presence now as I type. That really makes me feel good knowing I was looking for God although I was in darkness. I believe this prayer took place in April 1993.

Because of signs and wonders I was interested in Yoruba. This is how so many people get into false religions although they were Christians. However, I want to add this: these Christians who have left the Lord for Yoruba and other religions were in dead churches. Dead meaning that the Spirit of the living God did not move within these churches. There is no way you can have an encounter with Jesus and just walk away from Him to serve other gods. Notice in Yoruba; I would have been serving an angel (Orisha) and not God. Moreover, we were honoring and worshiping our ancestors too. After the Lord gave me the truth about Him which was in August 1993, I was so happy once I knew with all confidence that I had the true and living God in my life." From my book, "RUNNING THROUGH THE DARKNESS. The Story I Don't Want To Share" page 48 paragraph 2.

    I experienced Jesus before I gave my life to Jesus. Some of you reading this book believed Jesus is the Son of God without experiencing Him which is wonderful. As for me I needed more because of my background. I already didn't believe the bible, and I saw signs and wonders in the Yoruba religion. As you just read, there are plenty of Christians leaving Christianity because they experience the power in Yoruba and I experienced the power in Yoruba too, but it wasn't enough for me to embrace Yoruba. Why? My eyes have been open to the spiritual world my entire life. I saw things in the spirit my entire life from a child. If you're in Yoruba, Jesus can protect you from all Orishas if you come to Him. Jesus is the greatest power.

    I tasted Jesus before salvation and I tasted Him more and more as I grew in Him. To grow in Christ you must taste and see that the Lord is good. Psalm

THE ISSUE WITH ALL CHURCH LEADERSHP

34 verse 8. One taste of Christ and you will desire more and more and more. I feel sorry for Christians who are in dead churches. If the presence of God is not in your church then your church is dead. It's the Spirit of God that gives life. If you're not filled with the Spirit of God you do not have life. This is what makes us born again. If you're in a church that doesn't believe in being filled with the Spirit of God you need to leave this church. Pray for them that they believe, but you need to go where the presence of God dwells. It still won't be a perfect church, but at least God is in the midst.

To grow in Christ you must desire the sincere milk of the word of God. This is the basics in the bible. Do not read the Old Testament first. Study Matthew, Mark, Luke, and John. Read these several times. Learn about Jesus first. Then study Acts and the rest of the New Testament. Leave the book of Revelations alone. Just learn about Jesus for now. See how He cared, how He loved, and how He carried Himself. It's very important you have a good foundation on the basics. If you're at a great church they will already have a foundation class available. You can also find these type of videos online. Here's a note for your safety. If Jesus said it believe it. There are people who teach against certain things Jesus said. Do not believe these people. I don't care who they are. Believe what Jesus said. Watch out! My book, "Tainted Influence. Identifying Prophetic Truth & Error" gives a thorough teaching on these types of Christians and how to identify false prophets & false teachers.

While you're studying Jesus and the basics, you need to learn how to give God praise and worship at home. Play some praise and worship music at home. Lift up your hands unto God and open up your mouth telling God how good He is. Give God thanks for another day alive. Give God thanks for your life and family. Give God thanks every day. Here's an important verse, "But thou art holy, O thou that inhabits the praises of Israel." Psalm 22 verse 3. God dwells in your praise. God deserves your praise. Your praise should never be held back because you don't feel like it. Life can be very hard at times. Bad things happen. I've been there. I praised God through the passing of my father, my two sisters, and others. God is worthy of our praise at all times. He deserves it. Make up your mind to give God praise continually.

"I will bless the lord at all times: his praise shall continually be in my mouth." Psalm 34 verse 1.

"I will extol thee, my God, O king; and I will bless thy name for ever and ever." Psalm 145 verse 1.

"Praise ye the Lord: for it is good to sing praises unto our God; for it is pleasant; and praise is comely." Psalm 147 verse 1.

Study Psalm 149 and 150. Men, it's ok to give God praise. It's not gay. It's not feminine. Praise God in your masculinity. Be your authentic self while giving God praise. Second Samuel chapter 6 verse 14, "And David danced before the Lord with all his might;" Remember God dwells in your praise. Your presence sitting in church looking hard is not giving God praise. Ok, you're there. That's good, but that's not complete sir. You will have to open up gentlemen. Focus your thoughts on God. Think of you standing before God's throne in heaven. It's just you and God. Forget about everyone else surrounding you. This is personal. I'm telling you this from my own experience. I was that brother sitting in church hard looking around while the praises of God are taking place. Bring your hardness unto God in prayer and yield yourself unto Christ. If you're timid, bring all of your timidity to Christ. Get bold in your praise. Be strong in your praise. Amen.

Learn how to pray. When you start your prayer, acknowledge God with respect and honor. "Heavenly Father." "Lord God." "Eternal King." As you grow in Christ this will become easier. Bless Him before you make your requests. There are different types of prayers. You will grow in prayer. There are plenty of prayer books and online prayer videos. Always remember to honor God in prayer. As you grow and began to do warfare prayers, never be afraid of the enemy. Your good foundation on the sincere milk basics will help you in warfare prayers because you will understand who you are within Christ Jesus. The enemy is under your feet. You must know this and understand your position. You cannot bind the enemy if you do not believe. You must believe it and grow in it. There are plenty of online videos and books available. I have two books that will help you. "Enchanted. How Witches Attacked Me." and "Running Through The Darkness. The Story I Don't Want To Share." These books will teach you many things about witchcraft and your authority in Christ. You'll gain important knowledge to aid you in your walk with Christ.

Lastly you need to fall in love with Jesus. Anyone can give God praise. Anyone can join a church. Anyone can attend church regularly. Everyone will say they love God. Here's the hard truth: everyone cannot worship Christ. "But the hour cometh, and now is, when the true worshipers shall worship the Father in spirit and in truth: for the Father seeketh such to worship him. God is a Spirit: and they that worship him must worship him in spirit and in truth." John chapter 4 verses 23 & 24.

Worship: to honor and love as a deity.

You cannot fake loving God. God knows us better than we ever will. If you do not know the bible, can you say you love God? In order to love God you must learn about Jesus. "We love him, because he first loved us." First John chapter 4 verse 19. Learn about Jesus and appreciate the price He paid on the cross. When you're in God's presence, embrace the love He's pouring out on you. Focus on God in His presence. Allow God to love on you and receive His love. Yield your life unto God and allow God to freely have His way in your life. Humble yourself. What I've shared with you up to this point is called, "Seeking the face of God." I wasn't taught to do this. I'm not going to tell you to give up the world when you don't even know Jesus. All you know is the world. I'm teaching you to learn about Jesus. I'm teaching you to fill your new life in Christ with the things of God. There must be something tangible to replace the world in your life. So what's replacing the world? The kingdom of God. I'm putting you on a path that will help you fall in love with Jesus. As you fall in love with Jesus, you will worship Christ. As you fall in love with Christ, you will eventually have an amazing encounter that will change you forever. My encounter that changed me forever was when the Lord allowed me to see myself as He sees me. This encounter humbled me forever before the Lord. I used to believe if I stopped fornicating I would be a perfect person. I didn't see the other problems and issues I had in my life. This encounter was filled with the love of Christ coupled with me seeing myself in that same love I was feeling. When I say I saw myself, I saw myself from the eyes of God. Everything wrong with me was clear, but I saw it with the love of Christ. This was a beautiful event in my life and I will never forget it. We tend to think of the big sins and not the other things that are sin. All sin is wrong. All sin can send us to hell without receiving Jesus, and if we stay in sin after receiving Jesus without repentance we can still go to hell. Like I said before, Apostle Paul is my example. I can care less what these preachers and ministers are saying if it doesn't line up with the bible. "I therefore so run, not as uncertainly; so fight I, not as one that beateth the air: But I keep under my body, and bring it into subjection: lest that by any means, when I have preached to others, I myself should be a castaway." First Corinthians chapter 9 verses 26 and 27. A castaway is a Christian believer who did not make it into heaven. Once saved always saved is not biblical. You can miss the mark. Jesus gave the parable of the wheat and tares in Matthew chapter 13 verses 24 through 30. Before you ministers and other church leadership try to explain these verses in your own words, Jesus explained this parable in Matthew chapter 13 verses 36 through 43. Stop saying once saved always saved. Stop lying to people. If you are living in sin or living in any abominations like pastors with the first gentlemen etc., you will be a castaway. Heaven is a prepared place. It's not getting any bigger. It's prepared. You can be in ministry your whole life and end up in hell. "Not every one that saith unto me, Lord, Lord shall enter into the kingdom of heaven; but he that doeth the will of my Father which is in heaven. Many will say to me in that day, Lord, Lord, have we not prophesied in thy name? and in thy name have cast out devils? And in thy name done many wonderful works? And then will I profess unto them, I never knew you: depart from me, ye that work iniquity." Matthew chapter 7 verses 21 through 23. These people who didn't make it into heaven were in ministry. Let's look at iniquity. Iniquity: wickedness, unrighteousness, evildoing, infamy, depravity; gross injustice. Gross immorality. A grossly immoral act; sin. If you're married to the same sex your life is in continuous iniquity. If you're married and in adultery your life is in iniquity. If you're a fornicator and you're not trying to abstain from premarital sex your life is in iniquity. Guilty of sin and repenting is different from continuing to sin on a regular basis. I'm going to share a complete definition of fornication.

"Let's look at the word fornication in the blueletterbible.org because the devil has used the English dictionary definition to deceive Christian singles. Most English dictionaries say fornication is unmarried sexual intercourse. So many Christians took this thinking a penis inside a vagina is sin. Therefore we can give and receive oral sex and it's ok.

Fornication has three different meanings G1608 *ekporneuō*, G4202 *porneia*, and G4203 *porneuō*. The root word in all three New Testament definitions is "porn." The world of pornography contains everything sexual. Anything you do that brings a sexual orgasm is fornication. It's just like the world of porn. Porn covers everything that brings or gives an orgasm on all spectrums. Put the word porn in place of the word fornication in the bible. How do you feel now? All of you Christians who were doing everything else sexually, how do you feel? You have been deceived by the enemy. All sex before marriage is fornication, it's sin, and it's unclean. God has not called us to uncleanness. Our bodies are the temple of God. "Know ye not that your bodies are the members of Christ? Shall I then take the members of Christ, and make them the members of a harlot? God forbid. What? Know ye not that he which is joined to a harlot is one body? For two, saith he, shall be one flesh. Flee fornication. Every sin that a man doeth is without the body; but he that committeth fornication sinneth against his own body." First Corinthians chapter 6 v. 15, 16 &18. Listen, I didn't like it either. Let's go further.

Earlier I mentioned being "a real virgin." What's a

real virgin? Here's what I said in my book, "I'm Burning. Abstinence Tools For Single Christians" page 27 & 28.

If you're still a virgin reading this book, great! May the Lord keep you and may you flee fornication in Jesus name. Keep your virginity with all diligence and be that pure gift on your wedding night, amen? Amen! Be a real virgin. Don't be deceived by the flesh or deceitful sexual ideas like: "Well, if I only have oral sex I'm still a virgin." "If I have anal sex I'm still a virgin." All of these so called ideas and fleshly philosophies are not of God. If you have not had your penis inside a vagina, but it's been inside a woman's mouth and/or inside her booty hole, and if your mouth has been on a vagina licking, you are not a virgin. The same thing applies to you women who are receiving and giving oral sex, having anal sex, but your vagina has never been penetrated with a penis; you are not a virgin. This is deception. You all have been tricked by the devil. Those very thoughts to do these things came from Satan. Flee fornication truly means to flee all sexual activity. Plus, you are supposed to honor God with your bodies. Those sexual activities do not honor God and they defile your body. If you're guilty, well, repent and cease from it. Ask the Lord to cleanse you of all of those things. Be a real virgin and not a sexually polluted virgin. Amen? Amen! Anything that causes you to achieve or give an orgasm is sex. Just because you have not had sexual intercourse does not make you a virgin if you've done everything else sexually. You are deceived if you believe you can do all those things and still call yourself a virgin. You're lying to yourself and to those you keep telling you're a virgin.

I know that was pretty graphic for some of you religious folks. Get used to my transparent writing. In the mid-2000s I met a woman of God and she told me she was a virgin. I was so surprised and very curious how she remained a virgin. I wanted to know her story. This would be our only conversation. Although it appeared we were about to start a dating journey, I let this idea go. She was a singer, minister of music, and a pastor's daughter. She assumed I was like the men of God she's been dealing with before. I wasn't ready when she told me if I was her man, she would give me oral sex and anal sex until we got married. She wanted to receive oral sex from me. She believed fornication was vaginal sexual intercourse with a penis, and believed it was ok to do everything else. I couldn't believe my ears. She talked so freely about it like she knew I was going to agree with her. She was very sexually graphic. When I began speaking in vocabulary ending our conversation she quickly responded, "What? It sounds like you're not going to talk to me again." And I didn't. She wasn't a real virgin. She had her hymen, but she received orgasms and given men orgasms. A real virgin is a man or woman who has never had any sex of any kind ever. There's a man of God who used to be a homosexual and now he's a Christian. He told me he was a virgin. I asked, "How are you a virgin?" He replied, "I've never had sex with a woman." I just looked at him. I didn't understand his logic. This man had sex with men. That's still sex. He's not a virgin. If you were gay and now saying you're straight, you're not a virgin if you had sex with the same sex. Please stop the madness. Everything and anything that brings or gives an orgasm is fornication (porn). However you do it, if it brings an orgasm it's sex and sin. We are to live free of fornication. I know and understand how hard it can be for us. Nonetheless, this is the will of God." From my book, "BE CAREFUL WITH GOD'S DAUGHTER" line 1 page 47.

Iniquity can cause us to miss heaven. I'll never forget when a minister asked me, "Brother Marcus.

What's the difference between the kingdom of heaven and the kingdom of God?" I was a young Christian, but I answered correctly. I took a few minutes to think about it before I answered. The kingdom of heaven is where God dwells and the place He has prepared for His people. The kingdom of God is God's word in demonstration and activation in our lives. I didn't say it so polished back then. Why did I bring this up? For all the ministers of the gospel who will miss the kingdom of heaven, these ministers will still function with the kingdom of God in their ministries. These ministers will teach, preach, prophesy, and cast out devils. This is the kingdom of God being at hand. Once God anoints you to do a work for Him, He will not remove His anointing. Even if you decide to sin, God will not remove His anointing. God will use you to save others and say to you one day, "Depart from me your work was in iniquity." These ministers truly believe they are really ok because God is using them. God is faithful to His work He called you to do even though you're not living according to God's word. You will hear God telling you to repent, but you didn't listen. Once you've made up your mind to stay in sin while you're in ministry, God will turn you over to what you desire. You might be reprobated. If you're not reprobated you need to repent and turn from it. Seek healing, seek deliverance, be purged, and washed by the blood of Jesus. Iniquity should not be within the church leadership. "And because iniquity shall abound, the love of many shall wax cold." Matthew chapter 24 verse 12. Could this be the reason why the love is not present? God is faithful, but if we die with iniquity in our lives we are not going to heaven. The lake of fire will be our reward. All the ministers who are saying hell isn't a real place are wrong. Jesus says hell is real. Luke chapter 16 verse 23. Stop listening to these delusional voices in church leadership. Either you believe the bible or you don't.

"If you say you are a believer of the bible, you are saying that you believe the entire bible. You cannot believe certain parts of the bible and reject other sections of the bible. God's thoughts are not our thoughts and His ways are not our ways; you can read it for yourself in Isaiah chapter 55. God is who He is and whatever He does is right even if we don't understand His way of doing things. This is how many people of God end up in error although they started their walk with God correctly. You cannot build a doctrine off of a few scriptures. How can you only believe certain sections of the bible and negate other sections of the bible, but call yourself a Holy Spirit Christian believer? I can boldly say that you do not have the Holy Spirit and that you are a deceiver not a believer. This is why we have so many denominations today throughout the world, and why we have so many man-made, fleshly, and demonic doctrines. Furthermore, I would like to add that it's amazing that we all have the same book, but do not see eye to eye about its contents. This is why we all need to be filled with the Holy Spirit / Holy Ghost so God can teach us exactly what He means in His word. Without being taught by God we can all be in error concerning the bibles pure meaning. Even the people of God who sincerely live for God can eventually walk in doctrinal error if we are not careful.

In the book of Isaiah chapter 28 verse 7, you read where the priest and prophet have erred in vision and judgment. Verse 9 says, "Whom shall he teach knowledge? and whom shall he make to understand doctrine? them that are weaned from the milk, and drawn from the breasts." The next verse continues with, "For precept must be upon precept, precept upon precept; line upon line, line upon line; here a little, and there a little:" Line upon line and precept upon precept is saying how the word of God connects and confirms other scriptures and verses in the bible. Sound doctrine is solid biblical instructions, teaching, and messages that line up with other scriptures in the bible. Although some Christians don't believe in taking one verse from a chapter and using it with another verse from another book of the bible, using a line of scripture with another line of scripture is perfectly ok. But always remember whatever you are teaching must not contradict other scriptures and books in the bible. All pastors, apostles, teachers, evangelists, prophets, ministers, bishops, deacons, and clergy must be skilled in the word of God and be weaned off the milk of God's word. God can teach His knowledge and sound doctrine to those who are mature enough to receive it. If you don't even understand the basics of the bible (the milk), you can forget about operating and teaching sound doctrine (the meat)." From my book, "Tainted Influence. Identifying Prophetic Truth & Error" paragraph 1 page 128

Lgbtqia churches have the Queen James bible. You are on thin ice. Now add this to what you just read. Revelation chapter 22 verse 18 & 19, "For I testify unto every man that heareth the words of the prophecy of this book, If any man shall add unto these things, God shall add unto him the plagues that are written in this book: And if any man shall take away from the words of the book of this prophecy, God shall take away his part out of the book of life, and out of the holy city, and from the things which are written in this book." You changed God's word!

To all church leadership taking verses away from the bible, you will not make it into heaven. Your name will be removed from the book of life. You will be with the enemy in flames. I said it. I'm not apologizing. If you're angry right now you are angry at God. Take this up with Jesus. Like I said to you new Christians believe the bible. Believe the entire bible. There are certain things in the Old Testament, like sacrificing animals, that we no longer are required to do. This is why I tell you to study the New Testament first. You need a good foundation on Jesus. Please get my book, "Tainted Influence" to sharpen your knowledge about false teachers in church leadership. Now let's move on.

Your growth in Christ will have many moments where you will be excited. When you see yourself growing you will develop the fruit of the Spirit. Galatians chapter 5 verse 22 & 23. As you grow things you didn't understand will become clear and this will give you great joy. I tell you this from my own personal experience. Another thing that will take place as you grow will be the development of your spiritual gifts. First Corinthians chapter 12. Here's something I want you to know now before it happens, or it may be happening in your walk with Christ already. God will allow you to start discerning the leadership at your church. When this first happened to me I was in disbelief. My first reaction had me thinking I was wrong, but I wasn't. As I spent time with God I learned He wanted me to intercede for them. Intercession is when you are praying on the behalf of someone other than yourself. You're praying for grace, deliverance, or what ever it is that they need. What you see is not for you to spread all over your church or online. God is trusting you with this information. The same grace you would desire someone to have for you is the same grace you should show toward them as you intercede on their behalf. Continue to honor and respect them in their position. Remember no one is perfect and there is no perfect church. Struggling with sin is different from continuing in sin. They could have a stronghold that needs to be destroyed or a need to go through deliverance. Nonetheless, intercede on their behalf and do not think you're better than them because you see a fault in their life. You have faults too. Remain humble as you grow. Trust me, you will need someone interceding for you one day. As you grow the enemy will target your life, and you will need prayer from others outside of yourself.

Now if you feel like you're better than them, you have now crossed over into a character flaw called "self-righteousness." Most self-righteous Christians are those who have a good level of freedom and deliverance in their lives. Self-righteous Christians can become full of pride and walk in a very arrogant attitude. Self-righteousness Christians need to humble themselves under the mighty hand of God. You're not better than anyone else. The liberty and deliverance in your life was given by Jesus. You didn't do it. Jesus did it. Always remember, "Pride goes before destruction, and a haughty spirit before a fall." Proverbs chapter 16 verse 18. Don't ever think you're better than anyone else. What ever state the church leader is in remember to consider yourself. Show them the love you desire to receive if it was you in that condition. Walk in love. Do unto others as you would have them do unto you. Matthew chapter 7 verse 12. Amen.

Here's something you need to know. As you grow in the Lord, everyone in your church will not celebrate your growth. As I grew in the Lord and my eyes started opening to see things in the spirit realm, many in the church leadership shunned me. Some were jealous of my gifts from God. When I asked them questions about the things God was showing me they didn't want to answer. They would avoid giving me the information I asked for. At the time I didn't look at it how I'm writing it today. I thank God for those that did give me the answers I was looking for. When you're growing in God you are excited to learn new things. It's so wonderful when understanding of the word of God happens. It's amazing when God opens our eyes to more of His word. It's sad that some church leadership will not help certain people in their church continue to grow. Why? Some of them think you want their position in the church. Personally speaking, I really don't desire to be in church leadership again. I've been there and done that several times. I've been the head of the men's ministry. I've been an armor bearer. I've been a praise and worship leader. I've been the dance ministry leader. I know what's it's like to be shunned. If you are shunned by the church leadership, this includes your pastor, keep your eyes on Jesus. Just know that Jesus didn't shun you. Jesus received you and you are still in Jesus hands. Do not let your church leadership cause you to leave Jesus. Do not backslide. Stick with the Lord. Being shunned can hurt very badly. Especially if it happens with someone you look up to in the church leadership. My book "A Pastor's Mistake" is primarily about what I experienced with a pastor. This pastor was brutal and abusive over the platform. It's a big book with lots of documented issues captured. I had a journal and I recorded live church services. The reason I started recording live church services was because our church did not record the praise and worship. I wanted the entire service, but I also captured my pastor attacking me in front of the entire church. Prophecy controlled my life and when God let me see my pastor was wrong, I was humbly relieved. I was made to look like the devil, but God redeemed me and vindicated me. I honored my pastor anyway. I honored my pastor because it was right. Just because you're the pastor doesn't mean you are always right and it doesn't mean you can never mess up. Your pastor can commit sin and your pastor can fall. Your pastor is not perfect. Honor your pastor regardless.

"It's a beautiful thing to see a pastor say, "I apologize." or "I am wrong.", in front of the entire church. It's not a bad thing to apologize; it's a good thing to apologize. It's comforting to see a pastor acknowledge a transgression. Pastors make mistakes. Pastors are fallible. A pastor can fall into sin and commit sin just like any of us. Stop looking at your pastor as if he/she does not have any problems, faults, weaknesses, sins, and have it all together. If you study the word of God you will notice that God called plenty of people who had many problems and many weaknesses. We all have weaknesses. Yes, your pastor has weaknesses. Your pastor is not perfect. Do not be surprised if your pastor makes a mistake. Don't be shocked. All have sinned and come short of the glory of God. I pray the mistake is not something criminal. God will still love the pastor and God will forgive the pastor even in his criminal sin. However, if you do the crime you will be doing some time in prison. God says do not suffer as an evil doer." From my book, "What To Do When You Know Your Pastor Is Wrong" Line 2 page 99.

My first book was 2 books in 1. They are now 2 separate books. After I wrote this book many people came to me sharing their horror stories of how pastors did them. I connected with other authors who wrote similar books. God told me to write the book and I didn't want to do it. I didn't want the world to know what happened to me. It was too painful to share. This book you're currently reading is number 18 and I have more books to come. Write your story. I wrote my first book in tears, but it's helping many people who was hurt by their pastor.

To you new Christians, and young Christians, always honor the church leadership because of God. Even if any of them act a fool with you, do not retaliate. Take it to God in prayer. If they have the Holy Spirit / Holy Ghost, God can speak to them and tell them they are wrong. There are some who are stubborn and full of pride who will not apologize. Don't worry about it. I've never received and apology from certain church leadership and it's ok. I forgave them without their apology. I want to make sure my heart is pure towards God. I do not desire to hold any grudges because I do not desire to miss heaven. I recall when a praise and worship leader walked up to me saying, "I love you, but I don't like you." Then they walked off. I smiled. I didn't hold on to it. I let it go. You never know who may have an issue with you in church leadership, but you must respond in a way

Jesus will be pleased. If you need to repent, it's ok, repent and get it right with the Lord. Here's an example. Right in front of the pastor's wife I let a woman of God have a piece of my mind in the church. Yes, I did. This woman had a jezebel spirit and I was fed up with her. I kept complaining to our pastor and his wife, but they did nothing. I called her out in front of everyone. I was openly rebuked immediately for doing it while I was yet talking, but I was so happy I got it out. I apologized, but I really meant what I said and everyone knew I meant it too. I asked God to help me repent because I meant what I said. It took some time, but I finally felt bad for what I said and sincerely repented to God. This person wanted my position in the church. This situation was a very sad one. It will be in a book with all the details one day. You know what? I'll put it in the next chapter. As you grow in God, do the best you can when negative things arise and know you can always go boldly before God's throne of grace for help in the time of need or for the forgiveness of sin. God loves you and that's why this book was written.

As you grow in God you could possibly outgrow some friendships and outgrow some social circles. Why? When you delight yourself in the Lord and you're beginning to really love Christ, the desires of your heart are going to change. How? God will make the changes for you as seek him and spend time in His presence. As your heart becomes filled with the word of God you're not going to see things the way you used to see them.

I do not apologize for the word of God. We as Christians must seek the Lord. We must spend time in the presence of God on a regular basis. Going to church is good, but going to church and seeking God is better. "But seek ye first the kingdom of God, and his righteousness; and all these things shall be added unto you." Matthew chapter 6 verse 33. Seeking God first will bless your life with more of God. Do you really want to know God? "Blessed are they which do hunger and thirst after righteousness: for they shall be filled." Matthew chapter 5 verse 6. "Draw nigh to God, and he will draw nigh to you." James chapter 4 verse 8. If you would only seek the Lord, He will make sure you find Him, but you must seek the Lord. God will not force you to spend time with Him. Religious people do not spend time with God outside of church. They can quote many things they heard over the years in church, but they have not spent anytime seeking the Lord. I have corrected many religious people with things they are trying to quote in the Bible. Why say things you think are in the bible? "You make one step and God will make two." Not in the bible. "God don't like ugly." Not in the bible. Please seek the Lord.

Another thing you may experience as you grow are people who might be jealous of your growth. These people will probably be members of your church who are not in the leadership. I remember when I was asked to pray openly at church and I prayed in tongues before I prayed in English. To all pastors and ministers who teach against speaking in tongues, you are taking away from the word of God. When God filled me with His Holy Spirit I spoke in tongues as He gave me utterance. No one taught me. No one said repeat after me. "I understand that every church is not the same. Some churches don't believe in speaking in tongues. Some churches don't believe in prophecy. Some churches don't believe in women preachers. Some churches don't teach on seeking God, and some churches never preach or teach against sin. Some of you reading this book are shocked. Some of you never knew these things were written in the bible. I don't understand why pastors refuse to teach certain things in the word. If you don't believe or teach the entire bible, are you a partial son or daughter? Are you halfway on the road to heaven? Is God your half Father? Are you all in, or not?" From my book, "BE CAREFUL WITH GOD'S DAUGHTER" page 93 paragraph 1 line 15. If you're at a church teaching you not to believe things in the bible, you need to find a new church. If it's in God's word believe it. Being filled with the Holy Ghost is a real experience. It's very real. To everyone who is teaching against being filled with God's Spirit, what is your problem? How can you not believe? Why don't you believe? You are taking away from God's word. Revelation chapter 22 verse 19. Stop it. Repent and believe. Repent for teaching people to be unbelievers.

Like I was saying, there could be people jealous because your growth in Christ is causing you to be recognized by your pastor or church leadership. I've been there. When I was invited to sit with our pastor in the pulpit they were really upset about it. Stay focused on God as grow and do not let those jealous saints bother you. Stay focused on Jesus. Pray for them.

As you grow there could be some people who keep bringing up your past to people within your church as if that's going to stop you from growing. They are thinking wrong. Be bold when you testify of the goodness of God. Be bold when you share how God brought you out. Be bold when you share the things you no longer do thanks to Jesus. Don't be ashamed of your past. Jesus loved you so much He died for your sins. Everyone bringing up your past also has a past of their own. Jealously is a terrible fruit in the House of God.

As you grow in Christ your calling will be revealed to you at some point. Once you know your calling keep seeking God. You may not want to share what God revealed to you just yet. There will be many Christians in your church that will not agree with what you said your calling is and won't believe you heard from God. Some will boldly say you didn't hear from God and others will say that's not what you're called to do. Then they will tell you what you're called to do. This may not happen to you, but it did happen to me several times. Be prepared new Christians and young Christians. Amen. Stay focused. On the flip side of this, I've witnessed other new Christians join the church and they are received greatly. They are not rejected or shunned at all. This can be disheartening if you were shunned or rejected. If you didn't know you were shunned or rejected, you will soon recognize it after witnessing new Christians treated better than you. If this is your situation you're going to run to God and God will use your situation to cause you to grow in Him. If you're hurting because of this situation, cry out to God in prayer and tell Him exactly how you feel. Release your feelings to Christ. If you're rejected by your church leadership this situation can and will break you down. You may fight just to go to your church. You may debate with yourself if you're attending your church services and social events. I've been here in this place and because I ran to God He maneuvered my feet. He ordered my steps and caused me to grow as He led me through these situations.

Every situation in your life will be an event to cause you to grow in Christ. Whether it's situations on your job, things that happen at social events, and family issues, there will be many things in your life the Lord will use to cause you to grow. What fruit does this produce? Godly character.

"There is no shame like being openly rebuked when you are innocent and do not deserve the correction. If this is your situation you must maintain Godly character at all costs. With everything that's within you walk in the fruit of the Spirit. "But the fruit of the Spirit is love, joy, peace, longsuffering, gentleness, goodness, faith, meekness, temperance: against such there is no law." (Galatians chapter 5 verses 22 and 23) There is no law against how much fruit of the Spirit you can produce in your life. The more fruit of the Spirit the better. You can produce as much of this fruit as you desire. If you haven't developed some of the fruit, ask the Lord to help you develop the fruit you lack. Even as a fruit tree takes time to produce its fruit it will take time to produce the fruit of the Spirit. Nevertheless, whatever character you've displayed in your church up to now, as long as it's positive, you must maintain your true personality and identity as much as you possibly can. Do not change who you are in any capacity because of your situation unless the Lord directs you to do so. Please know it's truly the Lord directing you and not your own human intelligence.

Any change in your character will be recognized by those closest to you and by those with discernment. You do not want to do anything that will expose your situation with your pastor. If you are a leader in the ministry you must stay on your assignment and not express your negative feelings about your pastor to others in your church. This means absolutely no phone calls to your fellow church leaders, no phone calls to the laity, and no calls to people who do not attend your ministry; not even your own family. This applies to everyone in the church. By all means please do not post anything on social media about your pastor or your situation. Please don't even post hypothetical things trying to make it look like it's someone else's situation and not your own. Your Godly character must also be displayed on your social media and internet platforms." From my book, "What To Do When You Know Your Pastor Is Wrong." Chapter 4 "Maintaining Godly Character" Page 26 paragraph 1 & 2.

God will use every situation, event, and circumstance to cause you to develop His character in your life. You may not handle all of these situations correctly. You may have to repent and apologize to some. Remember that "And we know that all things work together for good to them that love God, to them who are the called according to his purpose." Romans chapter 8 verse 28. Even when you have to ask God for forgiveness it is working for your good. There are times when it may seem like things are a setback, and they probably are truly a setback, but it's still working for your good. Stay encouraged with your walk with Christ. Growth in Christ is not always easy, and you may experience things you didn't desire to happen, but it is still working for your good. In my 30 years I've experienced many things I couldn't have imagined experiencing in the church, but I kept seeking God through each situation and he directed my steps. God was so faithful to me. I was not perfect in every situation, but I learned from how I handled the situation and God revealed what I should have done. Even when I committed sin I learned from my mistakes as I sought the Lord. It caused me to humble myself even greater.

Your growth in Christ will be a very interesting journey. Enjoy the presence of God. "Thou wilt show me the path of life: in thy presence is fullness of joy; at thy right hand there are pleasures for evermore." Psalm 16 verse 11. Fall in love with the Lord and run to Him with everything you experience in life. Tears will happen on this journey, but there will be lots of joy as well. Be encouraged as you grow and learn more of Christ.

| Chapter Three |
Maturity In Christ

Maturity in Christ should be a prerequisite in order to be in church leadership. "And he gave some, apostles; and some, prophets; and some, evangelists; and some, pastors and teachers; for the perfecting of the saints, for the work of the ministry, for the edifying of the body of Christ: till we all come in the unity of the faith, and of the knowledge of the Son of God, unto a perfect man, unto the measure of the stature of the fulness of Christ: that we henceforth be no more children, tossed to and fro, and carried about with every wind of doctrine, by the sleight of men, and cunning craftiness, whereby they lie in wait to deceive; but speaking the truth in love, may grow up into him in all things, which is the head, even Christ: from whom the whole body fitly joined together and compacted by that which every joint supplieth, according to the effectual working in the measure of every part, maketh increase of the body unto the edifying of itself in love." Ephesians chapter 4 verses 12 through 16.

Honestly, it takes maturity to understand the fullness of these verses you just read. "Unto a perfect man" simply means that you have reached maturity. You are no longer immature as children who are tossed to and fro by every wind of doctrine. We've seen this often and we are probably guilty of being tossed to and fro. What do I mean? There's a conference coming to your city by a big name minister. You attend. Then another one comes and you also attend. Yet, you do not attend events by your own church. You feel as if your church isn't on the cutting edge of biblical knowledge and revelation so you are moved by other ministries thinking you're missing something. This is being moved by winds of doctrine. Your feet are running to hear other messages by other ministers and this could lead you to being tossed to and fro. As long as you're hearing the true pure word of God you will be just fine. Now that we have social media it makes it easier to listen to so many different ministers across the globe. I do not listen to everyone. There are ministers I used to listen to a lot, but I do not listen to them any longer. I did not make a conscious decision to stop listening to them. It doesn't mean they are teaching bad doctrine either. As I matured in Christ, my ears were not opened to every voice in the body of Christ. Every voice is not a pure voice. Notice Apostle Paul talked about doctrines that are cunning craftiness by the sleight of men who are deceptive. This doesn't mean they are teaching the bible falsely, but what it does mean is they are preaching a message with a purpose that's not of God. They have an agenda that is not within the purpose of God. It's a selfish purpose on their part. Maybe it's a message or prophecy to get money out of you. Maybe it's a message or prophecy that has undertones featured toward women to get them in bed. These types of ministers are not mature in the word of God. A mature Christian has a strong reverence for the Lord. Maturity brings you to a place where you desire to live right because of who God is to you. You desire to please the Lord because you love Him. Where I am right now as I write this book I am clearly abstinent. I was legally divorced in September 2021. Whenever my former wife and I was last sexually together was my last time having sex. Where I am right now I know to flee fornication. If I sin sexually there will be a strong chastisement from Christ. I do not have God's grace to hookup and smash from time to time. Like you've read in my other books, I love sex. Between a woman's legs is paradise. I love the female anatomy. The softer the woman the better. I love every inch of a woman's body.

"We live in a world that is filled with sex. Yet we are supposed to live godly, holy, and righteous. I've messed up so many times in my Christian walk. I've been on both sides of the coin. I know what it's like to stand and I know what it's like to fall. I know what it's like to be seduced and yes, I know what it's like to use a woman for sex on the Lord's side. I am so ashamed of many things I've done in the knowledge of Christ and I can truly say that no good thing dwells in my flesh. Loneliness and depression have taken me into some dark lustful places. I know what it's like to have a lonely horny pity party and crying out to God. A lot of our so-called lonely feelings are really just us missing sex in our lives. We call it lonely, but we are never truly alone. God is with us, but we are so thirsty and hungry for sex that we overlook this at times. I know what it's like to be angry at God because He wants me to wait until I get married to have sex. Yep, I'm just being honest with you." From my book, "I'm BURNING. Abstinence Tools For Single Christians." Paragraph 2 page 9. I wrote this book because books by popular ministers for Christian Singles didn't help me at all. These books didn't minister to me and they didn't deal with my single issues as a Christian. These books said what I should do, but did not give any information how to do it. I give you how and what to do information. I'm not proud of my body count and it would be much higher if I wasn't trying to please the Lord. In my 30 years as a Christian I have years of abstinence under my belt which I've done several times over. If you want to know about it all read my, "FROM WOMAN TO WOMAN" tell-all book series. I never did drugs. I wasn't a criminal. I wasn't a gangbanger. I was never a drug dealer. I've never been to jail. I never robbed people. As a black man I have been wrongfully put in some handcuffs several times in Chicago. I was released without incident. My issue was with women and guess what? I only wanted to be with 1 woman. I never wanted 2 or more women. My life is so unusual in my eyes. Now that I'm single again, I'm not currently dating or looking for a wife. I'm working on me as I write books to build the kingdom of God and I'm about to start writing fiction books for entertainment. When you're a new Christian and a young Christian, God gives you great grace as you are being purged and washed by the blood of Jesus. I don't expect babes in the Lord to stand and be sin free as they start out. Mature Christians should have less sin their lives. Not sin free; just less sin. The big mess-ups shouldn't take place in maturity. When it does happen this is why it's such a big shock. It's shocking because church leadership are supposed to be the examples to their congregation. It can happen if their focus is broken and they become prayerless. Everything you did to reach maturity in Christ must continue. Just like life goes on and there are no breaks, the spirit realm goes on and you should never take a break. You should never have that "I have arrived" attitude. Satan is looking to destroy us and he is not taking any breaks looking for a way to enter our lives. Satan is looking to get the church leadership to sin so members of the church will be discouraged and backslide.

Maturity should keep all church leadership in a humble place. Remember God gives more grace to the humble. If you're a church leader who becomes arrogant, full of pride, or self-righteous, you are setting yourself up for failure. Every fall in church leadership is not because of the devil. Sometimes God will allow church leaders to fall, and expose their sins, to humble them. Everyone in church leadership should be filled with the love of Christ. When church leaders lack the love of Christ, guess who is going to have the biggest problem with this? Exactly! Jesus is going to have the biggest problem. When church leaders are exposed for sin this humbles them and this puts them on their faces again toward Christ. There in the presence of Christ, on their face, they are reminded again of the love of Christ and His grace. I cannot make it without the grace of God. I'm humble because I would be sleeping with many women without God's grace. I'm humble because I understand it's God keeping me abstinent and not myself. Church leadership humble yourselves before you're caught up in a situation that humbles you.

Maturity in Christ comes with responsibility. God will reveal many people you are to intercede for in prayer. If you're filled with the love of Christ, He will show various brothers and sisters you are to pray for on a regular basis. Believe it or not, someone did this for you when you were a new and young Christian. God shows me the sins, strongholds, and struggles of Christians. Why? Because I do not judge people and I don't share it with anyone. If you're a gossiper and share this information to others, God will stop showing it to you. So if you're reading this and you no longer see the faults in Christians lives, this is why. You already know you're guilty. When we expose each other sins, God also exposes our sins. We reap what we sow in every area of our Christian walk. Love covers a multitude of sin. Love does not expose a multitude of sin. If you want to be covered, do not uncover. You want to reap being covered. I hated when my sins were exposed to the whole church. It only adds to the shame, guilt, and condemnation I was already feeling. However, when my sins were exposed it made me humble myself and run to God.

Reproach is something you will never want to experience. Reproach is when you get a bad reputation for sin, transgression, or iniquity. Whether you deserved reproach or not it hurts. I was lied on and this brought me great reproach. I talked about this freely in my book, "FROM WOMAN TO WOMAN VOLUME THREE" in the chapter "The Last Woman." I didn't deserve it. I was depleted and I ran to God to remove my reproach and to vindicate me. I eventually got to the place where I didn't care anymore. I got to the place where I was unbothered. I no longer looked to be vindicated. However, you may not feel like me. "Turn away my reproach which I fear: for thy judgments are good." Psalm 119 verse

39. "And she conceived, and bare a son; and said, God hath taken away my reproach:" Genesis chapter 30 verse 23. Believe me you will hate reproach. Now if your reproach is your fault, ask God for the grace to endure it. If you got caught in sin, deal with your reproach like a man or woman. Humble yourself, seek the Lord, endure, stand, and spend quality time in the presence of the Lord. Let the Lord lead you and order your steps from this current place.

King David had reproach. Second Samuel chapter 12. God exposed David in verse 12, "For thou didst it secretly: but I will do this thing before all Israel, and before the sun." King David's sin in verse 14 gave his enemies a reason to blaspheme God. When we see pastors caught cheating on their wives or their wives cheating on their husbands, pastors caught in homosexuality or with prostitutes, it gives the world, society, and non-Christians reasons to blaspheme Jesus. This is reproach. David was a man after God's own heart (First Samuel chapter 13 verse 14), but he yet committed adultery with Uriah's wife and murdered Uriah (Second Samuel chapter 12). Reproach can also come in other ways such as preaching or teaching demonic doctrine. Examples of this are in my book, "Tainted Influence." If you're a pastor, minister, or in church leadership, you must be very careful as you handle the word of God. First of all, you should be in prayer and spending time in the presence of God on a regular basis. If you are really mature in Christ, you should also be mature in the word of God. You should understand "sound doctrine" if you're mature. I'm learning many pastors, ministers, and church leadership are not teaching sound doctrine. Here's what I believe happens to these church leadership individuals. At some point they stopped spending time with God like they used to do. They began preaching things they already knew instead of receiving assignments in the presence of God to preach. One day they received a thought. They received this as a "new" revelation of God's word. Others hear a voice giving them a "new" revelation. Maturity in God should automatically examine this "new" revelation with and by the word of God. This is so sad when you see ministers walking in false revelations. I go in depth in my book, "Tainted Influence" and I will share multiple excerpts shortly. Listen y'all, there's safety in the simplicity of the word of God. We hear people of God in church saying, "That's deep." Here's what the bible says, "But God hath revealed them unto us by his Spirit: for the

Spirit searcheth all things, yea, the deep things of God." First Corinthians chapter 2 verse 10. You can live without the deep things of God. A good sound foundation in the bible is a beautiful thing. God's revelations will teach you more in depth about Himself and His kingdom. In the Old Testament God only shared His secrets with His prophets. Amos chapter 3 verse 7, "Surely the Lord God will do nothing, but he revealeth his secret unto his servants the prophets." Only God's prophets had His secrets and no one else.

"I would like to add one more piece of information about God revealing His secrets. You read the scripture in Amos about God revealing His secrets to His servants the prophets. I would also like to say that God will reveal His secrets to anyone He chooses to as well. In the book of Matthew chapter 13 verse 17 KJV, Jesus says, "For verily I say unto you, That many prophets and righteous *men* have desired to see *those things* which ye see, and have not seen *them;* and to hear *those things* which ye hear; and have not heard *them.*" The disciples were chosen to hear and see things that even the prophets of God haven't seen or heard. The disciples went on to be the apostles of God and have written most, if not all, of the New

Testament. The Apostle Paul is a perfect example of God revealing his secrets and revelations to someone who wasn't a prophet or in physical contact with Jesus. Paul wrote most of the books in the New Testament and because of his ministry we are Christians today." From my book "Tainted Influence. Identifying Prophetic Truth & Error" paragraph 1 page 158.

Nowadays, God can and will reveal His secrets and revelations to whomever He desires by His Spirit. It's not all centered around God's prophets. For a complete teaching on God's prophets read my book "Tainted Influence." All revelations come from the Spirit of God. If you're not spending time with God on a regular basis, how can you receive a "true" revelation from God? We already read Apostle Paul saying if he understood all mysteries, but don't have love he's nothing. Church leadership should focus on having the love of Christ and leave the mysteries / revelations alone unless God chooses to give it to you. Here's what I said in my book, "Tainted Influence."

"False doctrine and demonic revelations do not line up with the word of God. Any true revelation from God will line up with the scriptures in the bible. I am thoroughly grieved by many people claiming they heard from God, and the fruit of what they proclaim God told them is destructive to their soul, and to the souls of those who hear them. If God speaks to you it will line up with the scriptures in the bible. To make it plain, whatever God tells you, you will find it somewhere in the bible and it will not contradict bible scriptures. If it's not in the bible then there is a high probability that it was not God speaking to you. If it contradicts the bible it wasn't God speaking to you." – Tainted Influence. Identifying Prophetic Truth & Error page 115 paragraph 1 line 16.

There are revelations I received from God which I've never heard before from anyone. When I received these revelations I contacted men and women of God to tell them what I received. I wanted to know if they agreed with it or not. If you're proclaiming a revelation or mystery and you're teaching it openly, here's my question to you. How was this revelation / mystery being received? Let's look at your fruit from teaching this mystery. Did people get up and leave while you're teaching? Did lots of people resign their membership from your church? Was your church full and now it's empty? Did you lose your church? Are you still proclaiming this mystery / revelation? Who are you preaching to now? Did your inner circle get smaller? Why didn't you take this revelation / mystery to your fellow ministers first before you preached it? Did you seek the Lord about this mystery / revelation?

Now offended people can also leave your church in the manners I just written. However, offense and false revelations are two different things. lgbtqia are offended all the time because of the bible. Single Christians being told premarital sex is sin can be found offensive. There are many things in the bible that can offend people. Jesus taught things that people found offensive and multitudes walked away from Jesus. False revelations can cause you to end up in hell. Guess what? There are ministers who teach hell isn't real. How on earth can you say you're a Christian and do not believe hell exists?

"A preacher had a church at one time in the Lord until he started preaching false doctrine. I watched him as he was interviewed on a television program and I heard it in its entirety. He proclaims that no one is going to hell and that everyone is saved by Jesus' death on the cross and His resurrection. This former man of God is very wrong and there are people who are in hell at this very moment. Jesus Himself talked about the rich man who is in hell. (Luke chapter 16 verses 19 through 31) The book of Revelation chapter 20 verses 13 through 15 declare, "And the sea gave up the dead which were in it; and death and hell delivered up the dead which were in them: and they were judged every man according to their works. And death and hell were cast into the lake of fire. This is the second death. And whosoever was not found written in the book of life was cast into the lake of fire." Here is the hard truth: people are going to go to hell and then to the lake of fire. There are people who are not written in the book of life and they will not be with the Lord for eternity. Everyone who's name is written in God's book of life will spend eternity with the Lord. Everyone else will be in eternal flames because they did not receive the Lord Jesus Christ as their personal savior. Every time someone witnessed to you and invited you to their church that was Jesus drawing you to Him. Every time you rejected their invitation, you didn't reject the person you rejected Jesus. What God does is just because He is the supreme being. All statutes, rules, laws, powers, and anything and everything is subject to Him. God will have the final answer on judgment day. I don't want to go to hell and I don't want to see anyone else go to hell either, but to say no one is going to hell is unbiblical and a damnable lie that will lead many to the pits of hell.

This preacher has been bewitched by a spirit that is not of God and he is now preaching demonic doctrine. Remember saints of God, if anyone preaches anything that doesn't line up with the word of God it is a false or demonic doctrine. If you hear a voice speaking to you declaring it is God, whatever that voice proclaims must line up with the bible. God will not give you any information that doesn't line up with His word. This is how we know that preacher didn't hear from God. We in the body of Christ can clearly see that the preacher is wrong. If this preacher is correct then Jesus lied about the rich man being in hell, he lied about the lazy servant being cast into outer darkness, (Matthew chapter 25 verse 30) he lied about the man who came to the wedding who didn't wear a wedding garment who was also cast into outer darkness with weeping and gnashing of teeth, (Matthew chapter 22 verses 1 through 13) and we can throw the book of Revelations in the trash. Gnashing of teeth involves excruciating pain. Jesus didn't lie! Hell is very real and I found that out when I died at the age of 22. I didn't know Jesus and when I died I went to hell." From my book "Tainted Influence. Identifying Prophetic Truth & Error page 116 paragraph 1.

I recently wrote my book about my experience in hell. It's entitled, "RUNNING THROUGH THE DARKNESS. The Story I Don't Want To Share." At the time this happened to me I didn't believe the bible, and I fought against Christians. I debated Christians. I know hell is a very real place. It broke my heart hearing preaching telling everyone they are not going to hell. This is demonic doctrine. Doctrines of devils are mentioned in First Timothy chapter 4 verse 1. Doctrines of devils do not line up with the bible. Demonic doctrines are designed to keep you from operating within the kingdom of God. Once you are operating outside of the kingdom of God, you are no longer under the protection of the kingdom of God. You are now aligned with demons. You are on the devil's side now. You are living your life according to the devil's doctrine he has provided for you. The same way you used to live for God you are now living for the devil. It's written in the Old Testament and in the New Testament that homosexuality is sin. Leviticus chapter 18 verse 22 & Romans chapter 1 verses 24 through 28. You believed a demon who said homosexuality isn't an abomination. Jesus' death did not make homosexuality ok. Show me where it's written that it's ok? False revelations do not agree with the bible. If you're in a lgbtqia church you are not going to heaven because you are living by a doctrine of devils. The devil is going to the lake of fire and if you're living by his doctrine, how can you go to heaven? You're going to be with the devil for eternity. If you live for Jesus you will be with Jesus for eternity. Choose this day whom you will serve. Joshua chapter 24 verse 15. If you're married to the same-sex God does not honor it. If you're married and you and your wife are swingers, you are in adultery. It doesn't matter that you both are in agreement with it; it's sin. There are no loopholes with God. Any thought, voice, or supernatural experience you have with an angel of light does not change what God says in His word. You are now like Eve. She listened to the wrong voice and opened up herself to this idea outside of what God instructed. Church leadership be careful this isn't you. This is why it's important to have a good biblical foundation and why it's also important to keep seeking the Lord. Amen.

"Now we who are strong [in our convictions and

faith] ought to [patiently] put up with the weaknesses of those who are not strong, and not just please ourselves. Let each one of us [make it a practice to] please his neighbor for his good, to build him up spiritually." Romans chapter 15 verses 1 & 2 amplified Mature Christians should carry, encourage, love, and demonstrate the grace of God to weaker Christians. I could have said this earlier but I waited on purpose. I'm sure someone did the same for you. All of us are targets by the devil and his kingdom of darkness, but weaker Christians are easier prey. God requires strong mature Christians to build them up and edify them without judgment. We should not be living a life just to please ourselves. Always remember to consider yourself as you encourage them in their personal Christian walk. Amen.

Maturity in Christ means you have spent enough time in the presence of God that you understand how God speaks. There are many verses that say in one way or another, "He that has an ear to hear let him hear what the Spirit of the Lord is saying." A mature Christian should have an ear to hear what the Spirit of God is saying. There are some exceptions depending on what God desires to do. Here's my personal example. The year 2020 was a very painful year for most people. God did not speak to me concerning the things to take place in 2020. I was in a bad marriage and maybe this was the reason. I don't know. The church I was a member of did not prophesy anything about 2020 being a bad year at all. This church had many prophets and no one including our pastor said anything about what was going to happen in 2020. This disturbed me so much I went before the Lord in prayer, "God, why didn't you tell me what was going to happen in 2020? I don't understand why you didn't warn us. Why didn't you speak? Why didn't you speak to any of the prophets at our church? How come our pastor didn't see this coming?" I asked these questions in tears. I began to search the internet looking for someone who prophesied concerning 2020 correctly. My church was wrong. Every last one of their prophesies were wrong. Those words fell to the ground. They did not come to pass. This is not an attack on my former church. If you're wrong you're wrong.

"When a prophet speaketh in the name of the Lord, if the thing follow not, nor come to pass, that is the thing which the Lord hath not spoken, but the prophet hath spoken it presumptuously: thou shalt not be afraid of him." Deuteronomy chapter 18 verse

22.

I love these scriptures. If the Lord spoke it, it will surely happen and if He didn't speak it, it will not happen. So many pastors and prophets say, "You have to do your part to make the prophecy happen." When prophecy doesn't come to pass they always blame it on the person who received the prophecy. They tend to say, "You must have sinned or did something that was not in God's will for your life." Let's get real serious right now. How many of us have absolutely no sin in our life? The answer to this question is evident; all have sinned and come short of the glory of God." From my book, "Tainted Influence. Identifying Prophetic Truth & Error." Line 9 page 62. If God spoke it, it will happen. I was disappointed my church did not release the real word of the Lord for 2020. No one around me proclaimed what 2020 would be. After searching the internet, I found a video of a prophet dated December 31st, 2019. The Prophet Tony Rapu released the real word of God for 2020 and I cried in tears feeling relieved by God. Mature Christians should release sure words of prophecy. Mature Christians should have strong confidence hearing and speaking on God's behalf. "My sheep hear my voice, and I know them, and they follow me." John chapter 10 verse 27. If you're saying you're mature in Christ you should know the voice of the Lord. There can be times when you're under heavy spiritual attacks and overwhelmed to the point where you're not sure. What do you need to do? Seek God. It's the same method. Spend time with God even when you don't really feel like it. Seek assistance with your minister circles or even your inner circle of minister friends. Jesus has an inner circle which included Peter, James, and John. I've heard this my entire Christian walk about Jesus having His inner circle. I've heard this preached in many ways over the years. Everyone who preached or taught on Peter, James, and John justified having an inner circle. We call inner circles cliques these days. In the world they would be known as your squad, your crew, and posse for some of us old school people.

    Jesus had 12 disciples. He took time with all 12 to teach them the kingdom of God and to prepare them to establish His church. All of these men spent time with Jesus, but Peter, James, and John had something extra. On several occasions Jesus left the other 9 disciples and only took Peter, James, and John with him. Matthew chapter 17 verse 1, Mark chapter 5 verse 37, Mark chapter 9 verse 2, Mark chapter 14 verse 33, Luke chapter 8 verse 51, & Luke chapter 9 verse 28 are scriptures of Jesus bringing Peter, James, and John without the other 9 disciples. Was this really an inner circle? Could there be another reason why Jesus had Peter, James, and John with him? What if these 3 disciples needed this extra attention and experience with Jesus because Jesus knew they needed more than the other disciples for what He called them to do? Inner circles entail individuals who have things in common. I've been in the inner circles of pastors. Here's what I learned, but let me say I'm sure every pastoral inner circle will not be what I witnessed; at least I hope they are different. These inner circles weren't what Peter, James, and John (PJJ) experienced. PJJ witnessed miracles with Jesus which the 9 other disciples didn't witness. Jesus took time to expose PJJ to wonderful things like the Transfiguration (Matthew chapter 17), and told them not to say anything to the other 9 disciples in verse 9. This was something Jesus knew PJJ needed to experience to help complete His purpose in their lives. The inner circles I experienced talked about the faults, weaknesses, and sins of the members of their church. I even heard about the sins of ministers and the marriages that were in trouble. I was told not to say anything like PJJ, but at least PJJ could share what they experienced with Jesus at an appointed time unlike myself. What PJJ witnessed and heard with Jesus helped them with their Jesus given purpose. I didn't witness miracles in the inner circles. Once in awhile they talked about the things of God and were very excited as they shared scriptures with each other. These were the better times within the inner circles. I hated knowing people's business who didn't share it with me personally. Yet, they called it the inner circle. There was never a strategy to pray or intercede for the individuals who were talked about negatively. Why bring it up unless you specifically say let's keep them in prayer? I said all of that to say this: if your inner circles aren't building you up you don't need it. If your inner circle is not a place of strength, encouragement, healing, wholeness, prayer, deliverance, or intercession, you don't need it. Amen. God never answered my petitions concerning why He didn't speak to myself, my pastor, or the prophets at our church about 2020. I honestly hated being surprised how the world changed without a clue it was going to happen. It showed me I needed to seek God more. So what I was in a bad marriage and dealing with many other things in my life. I hated I wasn't informed by God and not hearing from God about 2020 humbled me. How many church pastors and church leadership didn't hear from God concerning 2020? I know it's a nice sized number. I'm very happy there were many who received the word of the Lord and proclaimed it. Let's continue with maturity in Christ.

Maturity is not always associated with the number of years you've been in a church. If you've been in a church 20 years, and have never read your bible at home you're probably not mature in Christ. A new Christian in your church who reads their bible daily, in a few years, will have more knowledge than the person in church 20 years not reading their bible. Maturity in Christ comes from seeking God's face. Maturity in Christ develops as you spend time with God. If you do not spend time seeking God you will not reach maturity. I've visited many churches full of religious people. Who are religious people? Religious people know church, but don't know God. These people know how to have church, or have some church, but they do not know the God they say they are serving. This is why religious people don't see much change in their lives. Since they do not seek the Lord and do not spend time with God, there is no tangible change in their lives. They can dress the part and look the part very well. They believe they are anointed, but the fruit of the anointing is not present. By the way, please stop telling everyone they have an anointing. Everyone has a gift, but everyone is not anointed. God doesn't just anoint anyone. When you receive God's anointing it comes with a purpose God desires you to fulfill. God's anointing is for the work of the kingdom of God. If you're not seeking God and spending quality time in God's presence, I can safely say you are not anointed. I received an anointing as a Christian single struggling with staying horny. God's anointing helped me abstain from fornication. I did not fornicate after receiving this anointing. I abstained 2 years until I was married to Kathy in my book, "A Pastor's Mistake." Here's what happened.

"As I sought the Lord, He began to do some new things inside of me. One day on my job, I was crying to God because my desire for a woman was burning tremendously and I needed the Lord's intervention. As I cried out to God, I experienced a gentle warmth come upon me. It was such a beautiful feeling and I started saying, "God, is this you?" Since the day this first happened, this warmth was always at my workstation. I have never experienced anything like this before. As I talked to my pastor about it, he let me know that God has given me an anointing. All I knew was that warmth felt very comforting and I welcomed it on my job. Before I was backslidden I spoke in tongues, but I didn't experience anything like this feeling. Moreover, I started seeing what looked like stars appearing and disappearing. I also started seeing dark shadows appear and disappear. I didn't understand what was going on with me, but I shared all of these events with my pastor. Pastor Davis explained, "Your gifts are being birthed and I will train you in your gifts." So, my pastor began explaining the different spiritual gifts I had and gave me the scriptures that backed up what he was saying. I was very appreciative of Pastor Davis. I was so happy God was doing wonderful things in my life, and it made me humble myself even the more." From my book, "A Pastor's Mistake" paragraph 1 page 35.

Why did I receive an anointing at work? I prayed as I worked every day at work. There were some sexy delicious looking women on my job. If I was a religious church person, who didn't spend time with God at work, I would not have received God's anointing at work. I desired to please the Lord by obeying His word. I know there are many single men of God who will not abstain. Abstaining is not a priority for them. Players in the House of God should not be a thing. I talked about this in my book, "BE CAREFUL WITH GOD'S DAUGHTER." Here's a portion of what I said.

"Here's what I told a brother in Christ who was bragging that he had five women he's sleeping with. I suppose he thought I was going to be impressed. I rebuked him. I guess the other men of God didn't rebuke him because he looked stunned by my words. Here's what I said after I rebuked him in the name of Jesus, "So, you got five women? (He said yes.) And you're sexing all five of them? (Yes.) Do you want a wife? (Yes) So, why should God give you one of His daughters? (Because I'm a good man.) What makes you a good man? You just said you're sleeping with five different women. (I know how to treat a woman. I will please her and make her happy. I'll take care of her. I'll be faithful.) Interesting. I'm not going to say God is not going to give you a wife since you're sexing five different women. God is faithful. (He's nodding thinking I'm about to say something good.) Well, God will give you a woman who's doing exactly what you're doing. (His face contorted. He's looking disgusted and repulsed.) See that feeling you're having right now, that's how you feel about yourself. (He got mad.) That disgusted look is how you feel about yourself. (No it's not.) Yes it is. Ok then, why is the thought of marrying a woman having sex with five different men nasty to you? (He didn't answer.) That's what you're doing. You would say she's a hoe right? (Right.) You're the hoe. You don't have five women. Five women have you. I'm not trying to make you mad, but you're a hoe. God is not about to give you His best and you're not His best for her." This brother is in position at a church. He's called on by his pastor to do things and to handle church business. This son of God wants a woman who's a holy angel and he's living like a lust demon. How many men of God feel exactly like this brother? Be honest with yourself. You say you want to be a husband, but you're a hoe. Not to mention you're going to reap these deeds you're doing. In the world players are respected, but you're not respected by God. The biblical term for player is whoremonger. What daughter of God wants a whore for a husband? No abstinence equals no self-control. You have no self-restraint. You're required by God to present your body as a living sacrifice, holy, and acceptable unto God which is your reasonable service. Romans chapter 12 v. 1. Men of God it's time to really live right. This is your warning." From my book, "BE CAREFUL WITH GOD'S DAUGHTER" Line 5 page 25.

When you're in church leadership you should not be engaging in sexual sin of any kind in any area of your life. The brother I rebuked sobered up for almost a year, but now he's back into sexual sin. At least it's not with 5 different women. He moved a woman into his apartment and they are not married. I don't understand. He knows he's wrong and he's still in church leadership. If you're in church leadership and in sin, you need to stop it immediately. You should know at least 1 minister who can pray with you to help you get free. There needs to be a strong urgency for you to get delivered and set free again. If you're in sin you are not in position to set someone else free through the laying on of hands. It's a sad situation when anyone in church leadership is living in sin. I'm not trying to be judgmental or critical. King David sinned and remained king, but he suffered the consequences of his actions. Please repent and turn from sin. There could be some severe consequences by the hand of the Lord. You already read about Jesus dealing with His church in the book of Revelations.

Please repent, seek the Lord, get delivered, and set free. Please come out of sin. Pray for this brother in Christ please. There should be a heart of repentance. There should be some Godly sorrow. Whenever you do not have a heart of repentance, not an "I'm sorry Lord" attitude, it shows there has been a change in your heart towards God. Where is your reverence for God? What caused your heart to change? Are you continuing in sin hoping that grace may abound? You don't respectfully fear the Lord anymore? Are you mature? In the book of Timothy chapter 3, you read about the qualifications for a bishop. Verse 6 & 7 says, "Not a novice, lest being lifted up with pride he fall into the condemnation of the devil. Moreover he must have a good report of them which are without; lest he fall into reproach and the snare of the devil." Although these verses are specifically concerning a bishop, this is truly for everyone in church leadership. Verse 8 talks about the qualifications of deacons. I love verse 10, "And let these also first be proved; then let them use the office of a deacon, being found blameless." The qualifications written in these verses applies to all church leadership and positions. Are you mature? Are you a novice? If you're a novice you are not equipped for church leadership. You're on your way to having reproach, the condemnation of the devil, and the snare of the devil. This is why everyone should be proved before being in church leadership. If you were never proven you should not be in church leadership. I was put in church leadership several times and I didn't believe I was ready. My pastor during those times said I was ready. I personally didn't believe I was ready. I didn't think I was proved yet. I share these situations in my books in full transparency.

    The book of Titus chapter 1 starting at verse 5 has the qualifications of elders and bishops. Now verse 6 says, "faithful children not accused of riot or unruly." Nowadays there are plenty of church leaders with children who are lgbtqia, in prison, drug dealers, etc.. It's amazing how the churches in the bible had strict rules and qualifications for church leaders. God has given the modern church tremendous grace. Look at Ananias and Sapphira. They lied to the Holy Ghost and dropped dead immediately. (Acts chapter 5) I am guilty of many things with Christ and I'm so grateful God's grace was so abundant on my life. I believe the grace of God is very abundant toward the modern church. Thank you Jesus. There are plenty of church leaders who wouldn't be in church leadership if

Apostle Paul was the overseer or if every church went exclusively by the biblical qualifications. I'm just saying. I'm not putting us down. We need to get it together people of God. If this book doesn't apply to you good for you. I hope you're humble about this and not full of self-righteousness. Just like there was 1 church of the 7 churches in the book of Revelation who the Lord was pleased with, there are churches today who the Lord is pleased with as well. 6 out of 7 seven churches had issues Jesus dealt with. Only 1 did exactly what Jesus desired of them. If you're in 1 of these churches today God bless you and continue in excellence. Pray and intercede for other churches please.

Church leadership if this is you please turn back to God. After you gave your life to Christ and began to grow in the Lord, you spent time in the presence of God. The Lord dealt with your sins in His presence. God revealed areas where you needed healing and deliverance in His presence. Now that you're in church leadership, the devil is going to target your life even greater. Your life should have been purged, cleansed, and washed as you grew in Christ. Strongholds should have been broken and destroyed as you grew in Christ. There should be a good level of liberty and freedom in your life at this point. The things you did to get to this point must continue. Keep praying. Stay in praise and worship. Study your bible. Spend time in the presence of God. Walk in the Spirit. If you stop now you can possibly lose ground. Those old habits can return. Temptation will seem like it's stronger or greater than before. God is the one who brought you to maturity. You didn't do it. In order to keep the liberty and freedom in your life you must keep seeking God and spending time in His presence. If not you can be caught up in sin and possibly be the next church scandal receiving reproach, under the condemnation of the devil, and snared by the devil. Then you would need restoration and I pray someone is there for you being Galatians chapter 6 verse 1 in your life.

Maturity in Christ involves greater levels of spiritual warfare. This is another reason why you cannot live in sin. As you grew in Christ you also experienced spiritual warfare. I didn't talk about it on purpose. Just focus on God and seek Him. That's what's most important. The devil is under your feet. The authority of Christ is on your life now and the devil doesn't have power over you anymore. However, sin opens the door for the devil to attack you. Get my book, "Enchanted. How Witches Attacked Me" to learn about the spirit realm and satanic attacks through witchcraft. As you grow in Christ you will learn your authority over the devil through Christ. Study Ephesians chapter 6, Second Corinthians chapter 10, First Thessalonians chapter 5 verses 8 & 9, and Romans chapter 8 verses 37 through 39 for verses on spiritual warfare. You mature people should already be aware and knowledgeable of these verses. Please remember this book is primarily for the new Christians and young Christians. You'll learn your authority in Christ as you continue to seek the Lord.

Let me share a story of a church leader attacking me. There was an ordained minister who proclaimed if Obama becomes the president of the United States, the mark of the beast will happen under his presidency. He did this on Facebook. I kindly and respectfully commented saying you're wrong sir. The mark of the beast will not happen if Obama wins. He commented and I responded. He blocked me. We had several mutual friends who showed me what he posted about me. He posted a picture of me and proclaimed I was a false prophet. This ordained minister was out to destroy my name. Well, I took it to God in prayer. Well, Obama won twice and no mark of the beast. He was under the snare and the condemnation of the devil. His false prophecy of the mark of the beast happening under Obama gave him great reproach. Our mutual friends saw it all unfold. Why did I bring this up? Too many times people in church leadership have pride. They do not want anyone to correct them or they cannot receive correction from anyone. Since I wasn't an ordained minister he felt like, "What can you tell me?" or "Who are you to tell me I'm wrong?" Well, if he would have had a humble disposition he wouldn't have reproach right now. He's no longer blameless. An example of an ordain minister being rebuked in the bible is Apostle Paul rebuking Apostle Peter. Galatians chapter 2 verses 11 through 14. The same Peter who was in Jesus' inner circle. Rebuke is the love of Christ. Correction is the love of Christ. "For whom the Lord loves He chastens, and scourges every son whom he receives." Hebrews chapter 12 verse 6. If God loves you He will correct you when you are wrong. Why do many church leaders have this prideful attitude as if they are never wrong? All of us should be open to correction and very humble when we are corrected. Correction is God's protection. If that ordain minister would have just listened to what I said to him he wouldn't have a tarnished reputation and reproach. We are all within the body of Christ and fitly joined together. We are all filled with God's Holy Spirit / Holy Ghost. Being in the church leadership does not make those in your congregation any less than you. There are verses saying we should honor you and reverence you because of the position you hold. I agree with this. "Let the elders which rule well be counted worthy of double honor, especially they who labor in the word and doctrine." First Timothy chapter 5 verse 17. Elders are within the church leadership. It says let the elders which "rule well." Ok, so there are elders that do not rule well. If you're not ruling well you may not receive double honor. You're not fooling Christ. However, I say to everyone in the body of Christ. Honor every position even when their character, actions, and preaching is questionable. Treat them with respect because of God. "And we beseech you, brethren, to know them which labor among you, and are over you in the Lord, admonish you; And to esteem them very highly in love for their work's sake. And be at peace among yourselves." First Thessalonians chapter 5 verses 12 & 13. Look what Apostle Paul said, "Know them which labor among you and are over you in the Lord." Church leadership your name and reputation is in your hands. How you act and conduct yourself is what the congregation, or social media following, will know about you. Whether it's the love of Christ or you have an attitude problem. Whether it's the grace of God or you have a lust problem. It's in your hands church leadership just like this ordain minister gained reproach by being openly wrong on social media. I wasn't attacking him. My actions weren't personal at all. I only said what God told me to say. "But the bible says rebuke not an elder. Why did you rebuke him?" (First Timothy chapter 5 verse 1) The Lord rebuked that ordained minister / elder. I was the available vessel. There are plenty of things I see online with church leadership and I do not address it unless God tells me. Contention with anyone can become spiritual warfare. Witchcraft is a real thing even in the church. Words are spirit. The things you say about people are spirits. "Death and life are in the power of the tongue." Proverbs chapter 18 verse 21. The minister who attacked me released evil words against my life, but he reaped what he sowed because he failed to have an "ear to hear" the voice of the Lord. Now his name and reputation is tarnished with reproach. If he only had an ear to hear the Lord he would have heard God speaking through my voice. However, he couldn't hear God through me. God was trying to save him from the consequences of his actions. I talked about this briefly in my book, "WHAT TO DO WHEN YOU KNOW YOUR PASTOR IS WRONG." I'll share a different excerpt shortly with what I'm about to talk about next. Let's continue.

Maturity in Christ should not have church leadership against other church leadership. I'm sure some of you have witnessed pastors preaching against other pastors. We have definitely observed this on social media. It's very sad. You think you're exposing your brother, but you're only making yourself and the body of Christ look bad. In addition, there are gossip podcast highlighting the issues in the church. Why? Here's my question. Is this edifying? Not at all. I cut it off. I don't need to hear all of the details. To everyone filled with the love of Christ this is discouraging and my heart aches seeing someone's sin openly exposed. The only contention I recall in the New Testament is Paul and Barnabas. Here's what I wrote.

"An example of this comes from the book of Acts. In chapter 13 verses 2 and 3 KJV reads, "As they ministered to the Lord, and fasted, the Holy Ghost said, Separate me Barnabas and Saul for the work whereunto I have called them. And when they had fasted and prayed, and laid their hands on them, they sent them away." We see here that God called Barnabas and Saul to work together in ministry. In verse 4 and 5 we see that Barnabas and Saul were sent by the Holy Ghost, and John also went with them. Now the Holy Ghost did not call John to the ministry that Saul and Barnabas were called to do, but he assisted them in their ministry for a short season. In verse 9 we see where Saul is now being called Paul. In verse 13 John left Barnabas and Paul, and returned to Jerusalem. God used Barnabas and Paul mightily from the time they were sent forth into ministry.

However, in Acts chapter 15 verses 36 through 40, things drastically change. The KJV reads, "And some days after Paul said unto Barnabas, Let us go again and visit our brethren in every city where we have preached the word of the Lord, and see how they do. And Barnabas determined to take with them John, whose surname was Mark. But Paul thought not good to take him with them, who departed from them from Pam-phyl'-i-a, and went not with them to the work. And the contention was so sharp between them, that they departed asunder one from the other: and so Barnabas took Mark, and sailed unto Cyprus; And Paul chose Silas, and departed, being recommended by the brethren unto the grace of God. And he went through Syria and Ci-li'-ci-a, confirming the churches." What's wrong with this picture? Well, first of all God called Barnabas and Saul/Paul to a specific work in ministry together. God did not call John (Mark) to the ministry of Paul and Barnabas. John assisted them for a season and left them, now he wanted to come back to their ministry. Barnabas wanted John to come back to their ministry, but Paul didn't want John back in their ministry. Barnabas and Paul had a very sharp contention over John who wasn't even called to work with them in ministry. Now this picture is very sad indeed. Two people who were called by the Holy Spirit to work in ministry together are fighting over someone who wasn't even called to work with them in their ministry. They had a serious fight over nonsense. Nevertheless, Barnabas chose John (Mark) and went on his way. Did Barnabas ask the Lord to take Mark? Well, it's not in the bible if he did. Therefore I conclude Barnabas was leading himself without the Lord's direction. On the other hand, we see in verse 40 Paul chose Silas being recommended by the brethren unto the grace of God. Paul chose Silas after getting counsel and specific instructions. But most of all, Paul chose Silas with the grace of God. Barnabas didn't have the grace of God when he chose Mark. The ministry of Paul and Barnabas, which God called them to do together, ended with a fight over Mark who wasn't even called to work with them in ministry. In verse 32 we see that Silas was a prophet of the Lord. However, with the grace of God, Silas took Barnabas's place in ministry with Paul." From my book, "WHAT TO DO WHEN YOU KNOW YOUR PASTOR IS WRONG." Paragraph 1 page 75.

If contentions occur, the major difference maker will be the person who moves forward in the grace of God. Most of these ministers and pastors attacking other church leadership is not operating in the grace of God. How do I know this? Well, look at the fruit of what's being detailed. Is it with God's grace and the love of Christ? Are they damning these people to hell? There's your answer. Where is the compassion for their soul to be restored and made whole? Church leadership take notes and everyone in the body of Christ as well. If you're not sharing situations and circumstances with the love of Christ to edify the body of Christ, you are wrong. You can now be considered an enemy of Christ. You're only making the body of Christ look bad. In return you are going to reap what you sowed by the hand of the Lord. You know what you're dealing with in secret. I know what I just said and I meant it too. Every church leader has at least 1 thing in their personal walk with Christ that should keep them humble with the Lord. I don't need to know you to proclaim this. I know the bible. Apostle Paul is my example and no one in the body of Christ alive today is greater than Apostle Paul. "And lest I should be exalted above measure through the abundance of the revelations, there was given to me a thorn in the flesh, the messenger of Satan to buffet me, lest I should be exalted above measure. For this thing I besought the Lord thrice, that it might depart from me. And he said unto me, My grace is sufficient for thee: for my strength is made perfect in weakness. Most gladly therefore will I rather glory in my infirmities, that the power of Christ may rest upon me. Therefore I take pleasure in infirmities, in reproaches, in necessities, in persecutions, in distresses for Christ's sake: for when I am weak, then am I strong." Second Corinthians chapter 12 verses 7 through 10.

Apostle Paul said he was given a thorn in his flesh by the messenger of Satan. I've never heard anyone preach on the messenger of Satan. This demon is like the angel Gabriel who is God's messenger. This is the angel that talked to Mary Jesus' mother. Gabriel stands in the presence of God waiting for Instructions and assignments. The messenger of Satan put a thorn in Paul's flesh. To make it simple, Apostle Paul was given a fault or a weakness which he asked Jesus to remove 3 times. Jesus said no and told Paul it's covered with His grace. Paul says he understood it was given to him so he would not be exalted above measure because of the revelations God has given him. God allowed it. God allowed the messenger of Satan to attack Apostle Paul with something that others can discern and see so Paul would not be honored above measure. Paul could not bind this demon because God allowed it. God did not remove it although Paul asked. God allowed it. Is it sitting in yet? Maybe the things you church leaders are dealing with in secret is to keep you humble and to remind you of the need for God's grace continually in your life. I don't need discernment to know you've got something in your life God is allowing to keep you humble. I don't care about your name or reputation.

You've got something in your life keeping you at the foot of the cross, and you're not greater than Apostle Paul. We are the fruit and labor of Paul's ministry. New and young Christians be encouraged no matter what you see or witness in the church. Know Jesus is real regardless of what you see others do. If I fall off and turn my back on Jesus, God forbid, Jesus is still real. All of us must endure until the end of our lives to be saved and spend eternity with Christ. I heard of a very sad situation. When I first gave my life to Christ there was a church mother who gave me a pack a-shirts after church. She whispered in my ear, "Wear these under your dress shirts to church." I was clueless why at first. I didn't wear undershirts at all. Not even outside of church. I was really clueless about proper church attire. This was the first gift I ever received in church. This same church mother spoke in tongues and sung often in our church. Many years later I heard some disturbing news. This same church mother near the end of her life stopped living for Christ. She started serving another god. This is so sad. At her funeral she had instructions to have this other doctrine preached. She left instructions to tell everyone what doctrine she now served. It was not Jesus Christ. I cried deeply for her soul. We must die in Christ to receive the eternal rewards in Christ. Keep your life in Christ until your last breath. "Jesus saith unto him, I am the way, the truth, and the life: no man cometh unto the Father, but by me." John chapter 14 verse 6. Jesus is the only way into heaven. Don't let anything you witness in the body of Christ cause you to change your mind. Jesus is very real. If you are involved in contention, witness contention, or view contention on social media, make sure you are directed with the grace of God or witness if the grace of God is administered or directed. If you are contentious without the grace of God you need to repent and apologize if necessary. We cannot live this life without the grace of God. It took grace to save our souls and it will take the grace of God to complete the purpose of God until our last breath. Outside of grace is the mercy of God. Outside of mercy is God's judgment. I thank God for His mercy when I did many things I knew were wrong. God had mercy on King David when he committed adultery and murder. "And Nathan said unto David, The Lord also hath put away thy sin; thou shalt not die." Second Samuel chapter 12 verse 13. David was forgiven before he repented of his sin. Show me where David repented before Prophet Nathan brought "rebuke and correction" to him? King David's actions were worthy of death. God told David through Nathan the prophet that he will not die. Just think…, this was before Jesus died on the cross. So many people think God didn't show any grace or mercy in the Old Testament. We saw what happened to King Saul. There was no grace or mercy with Saul's disobedience to God's. One had grace and mercy, and the other was judged by God.

"Look at how many times we've sinned against God. He yet loves us and He forgives us. Although we have disappointed God many times He constantly forgives us and He is yet faithful to all of our needs. Remember when David committed murder and adultery? The Prophet Nathan told David that God has pardoned his sin. Nowhere in the scripture do we read about David repenting of his murder and his adultery until his sins were exposed and corrected by God through the Prophet Nathan. God forgave David even before David repented. How many times has God forgave us of sin we took too long to repent of? We just don't know do we?" From my book "WHAT TO DO WHEN YOU KNOW YOUR PASTOR IS WRONG" Paragraph 1 line 10 page 53. Anytime God forgives us we should be more humble. Especially when we have done things worthy of God's judgment.

It should make us see the grace and mercy of God in more intimate ways. Ways that should keep us close to the cross. Never forget the price Jesus paid for your salvation. If you forget it, it could lead you away from Christ just like this church mother.

Once you've reached maturity you must watch as well as pray. It's not optional. You cannot practice sin and think everything is ok. You are now in a place where living in sin or opening up to sin can cause you to be bound by the enemy. Now is not the time to give in to the flesh. This is not the time to test the grace of God. If lust is fighting you to the point where you desire to sin you must humble yourself and be honest with God. With every temptation God leaves a way to escape. (First Corinthians chapter 10 verse 13) In times of weakness, and temptation, we must seek the Lord with sincerity for our escape route. With maturity comes understanding of things new Christians and young Christians do not understand. Now that you've grown to this point with Christ you know and understand the price for sin. Not all sin have the price I'm about to detail. Little things are covered by the grace of God and anything the Lord has given you to be a thorn to keep you humble. Outside of these things if you commit sexual sin, abominations, receive and walk in false revelations, preach another version of Christ that doesn't line up with the bible, or do things likewise, you can break your hedge of protection by God's angels. You will be opened up to the attacks of the devil and you can receive evil spirits that you will not be able to fight off. These evil spirits will bind your life. Apostle Paul could not bind or fight off the messenger of Satan because God allowed it. Paul knew his authority in Christ and when that didn't work he asked Christ to remove the thorn knowing Jesus answered his prayers. Paul did not do anything to deserve the thorn he received. He lived according to God's word so much that he needed a thorn so the body of Christ would know he's human and needs the grace of God like everyone living for Christ. In your case, you broke your hedge of protection and you no longer have the authority of Christ on your life. You must be in Christ to have his protection and authority on your life. David committed sexual sin and murder. God judged his actions, but David stayed king. There are cases when pastors committed sin and kept their pastoral office. They endured great reproach and lost many members of their church. Once you're in church leadership you are required to be a good example to the body of Christ. If there are things in sin that you wished you would have experienced, guess what? It's too late to do those things. When I got saved at age 22 I envied those who grew up in the church. It's amazing that many of them wished they were in the world and didn't grow up in church. This is why so many of them leave the church once they are adults. For some they do not make it back to the church. Some died in sin. They went to the wrong party and was shot to death. Others tried the wrong drug and died of an overdose. It's so sad. Maybe they repented just before they died. Why risk eternity for sin? Stay in Christ. If there is something you wished you did in sin take it to God in prayer and yield that sinful desire to the Lord. Ask yourself this question: why do I want to sin against God? Just think about it. Now that you're in church leadership you want to sin. Are you sure this is even your desire? Maybe the devil remembers what you desired to do and he's the reason you're thinking about it. If you're really mature you know the devil attacks our minds. Maybe these thoughts reminding you of what you wished you would have experienced in sin are from the devil. Did you even attempt to bind these thoughts and cast them down? Anyway, it's your soul. Now let's continue.

I want to talk to female ministers briefly. Do not listen to these men in church leadership telling you God didn't call you to be a pastor, teacher, apostle, evangelist, or prophet etc. Ladies of the Lord, do what God has called you to do. I know every verse these men use against you that Apostle Paul wrote. Apostle Paul also wrote, "For ye are all the children of God by faith in Christ Jesus. For as many of you as have been baptized into Christ have put on Christ. There is neither Jew nor Greek, there is neither bond nor free, there is neither male nor female: for ye are all one in Christ Jesus. And if ye be Christ's then are ye Abraham's seed, and heirs according to the promise." Galatians chapter 3 verses 26 through 29. Apostle Paul is saying clearly that no one is greater than the other in Christ. Men are not greater or preferred in Christ. We must all fulfil the plan of Christ for our life. You women sitting in churches doing nothing because of your pastor need to leave. If your pastor is saying, "If you leave this church you're going to hell." or "If you preach you're going to hell.", your pastor is clearly wrong. Apostle Paul said there is neither male or female in Christ, and we are both joint heirs according to the promise. These pastors and church leaders do not have the love of Christ nor do they operate or function with the grace of God. Who are you to tell someone not to teach or preach? You don't know the plan of God for their life. Especially when you already have a stiff disposition against women as ministers in church leadership. "Therefore, my brethren dearly beloved and longed for, my joy and crown, so stand fast in the Lord, my dearly beloved. I beseech Euodias, and beseech Syntyche, that they be of the same mind in the Lord. And I entreat thee also, true yokefellow, help those women which labored with me in the gospel, with Clement also, and with other my fellow laborers, whose names are in the book of life." Philippians chapter 4 verses 1 through 3. Apostle Paul shows how much he loves the church at Philippians as he starts chapter 4. Let's look at some word definitions.

Beseech: pray, petition, beg eagerly for; implore urgently:

Implore: 1. To appeal to in supplication; beseech:
 2. To beg for urgently: To make an earnest appeal

urgent: 1. Compelling immediate action or attention; pressing.
 2. Conveying a sense of pressing importance:

Apostle Paul beseeched Euodias and Syntyche to be of the same mind in the Lord. I only wished we had the background of what was really taking place in depth with these two brothers in Christ. After addressing these brothers in love and praying, petitioning, and eagerly begging Euodias and Syntyche to be of the same mind, Apostle Paul also entreats the "true yokefellow" to help those women which labored with himself and Clement in the gospel. Ministry is called labor. "For I am the least of the apostles, that am not meet to be called an apostle, because I persecuted the church of God. But by the grace of God I am what I am: and his grace which was bestowed upon me was not in vain; but I labored more abundantly than they all: yet not I, but the grace of God which was with me." First Corinthians chapter 15 verse 9 & 10.

Look at Apostle Paul's heart. I believe persecuting the church of God haunted him. He called himself the least of all apostles although he labored more than all of them. He didn't call himself the greatest apostle. I can safely say he is the greatest of them all. The grace of God on Apostle's Paul life was not in vain. Look at some of these ministers today adding new titles in the church that are not in the bible. You can't just be a prophet, apostle, bishop etc., you have to make your title and church leadership position sound bigger. Where is the humility and humbleness? "But he that is greatest among you shall be your servant." Matthew chapter 23 verse 11. Here's a question for church leadership across the globe: why does your church serve you and you don't serve your church? Jesus served His disciples. His disciples didn't serve Him. I'm not going to go any further with this. Let's continue with Apostle Paul talking to the church of Philippians.

Apostle Paul asked Euodias and Syntyche to be of the same mind and also the "true yokefellow." Yokefellow: a working companion.

An associate or companion.

Paul addressed the "true" working companions and associates in Christ to help those women who labored with him in the gospel. Apostle Paul also had a revelation that these women's names were written in the Lord's book of life. Women of God be encouraged today. Although these women weren't named in this epistle their names are in the book of life. They labored in the gospel with Apostle Paul. Obviously their mouths were open to preach and teach the gospel. You don't have to sit in silence in the church. "Let your women keep silence in the churches: for it is not permitted unto them to speak; but they are commanded to be under obedience, as also saith the law. And if they will learn any thing, let them ask their husbands at home: for it is a shame for women to speak in the church." First Corinthians chapter 14 verse 34 & 35. Let's look at verse 33, "For God is not the author of confusion, but of peace, as in all churches of the saints." Let's look at the last verse, "Let all things be done decently and in order." What was going on in this church? Confusion. What was the "law" Apostle Paul was talking about? Where is this law in the bible? Let's look at First Timothy chapter 2 verses 11 & 12, "Let the woman learn in silence with all subjection. But I suffer not a woman to teach, nor usurp authority over the man, but to be in silence." Well, all of these verses together don't make any sense. So women labored with Apostle Paul in the gospel and he asked other men of God to help them, and he says there is neither male or female in Christ. Well, which one is it?

"And Deborah, a prophetess, the wife of Lapidoth, she judged Israel at that time." Judges chapter 4 verse 4. Before there were kings in Israel, God ruled

His people with His judges. The judge held all the power in Israel. Deborah had a husband named Lapidoth, but God made her the judge. She was subject to her husband at home, but as judge her husband was under her authority with the nation of Israel. God ordained Deborah judge over His people. You men against women ministers, how do you feel right now? Do you have a problem with this? You should be mature in Christ and you should know Judge Deborah exists. If God allowed this in the Old Testament under the law of Moses and now in Christ there is neither male or female, why would God shut the mouths of women in every church?

As judge Deborah heard from God as she dwelt under a palm tree chillin' as the children of Israel came to her for judgment. (Judge chapter 4 verse 5) How would you men feel if you had to go to a woman for judgment? Are you angry right now? Did you throw this book as hard as you could? So we definitely see God ordaining a woman who is the ruling authority over a nation. Sounds like a pastoral or apostleship position. Barak was instructed by God through her to go to war and he didn't want to go unless she went with them to war. (verse 8) Barak needed her presence at war. Sounds like intercession and spiritual warfare to me. Deborah went with Barak and didn't have to go home to ask her husband if she could go to war with Barak. I'm very sure Lapidoth was a man of God and understood his wife's position as judge without contention.

Most churches are full of women and you're telling me that no woman can say anything in any church? These men say only men can talk in the church. Yet, Apostle Paul had women helping him in ministry and he addressed other men of God to help them with their ministry. Plus, their names are in the book of life. Let's make it make sense. What was going on in the church at Corinth? What was going on in Timothy's church? Each epistle was written for a specific reason. Each epistle (letter) was written for specific situations and circumstances. Those instructions were tailormade.

Who put the bible together? The short answer is the Catholic church. The translations are by Saint Jerome who chose the books that we know as the bible. Before the Catholic church put all of these books and epistles together in one book, they were all individual books. If I wrote you a letter (epistle), can you give that same letter to another person and tell them to abide by what I wrote? Of course not. So, what was going on within the church at Corinth? The Corinthian church had plenty of issues. We need to identify why Apostle Paul addressed this church to teach women to be silent. In First Corinthians chapter 11 verse 5, Apostle Paul is giving instructions to women who are prophesying and praying. In verse 13 Paul says, "Judge in yourselves: is it comely that a woman pray unto God uncovered?" Wait..., prophesying is speaking on God's behalf like Judge Prophetess Deborah. Praying is talking to God or making requests to God. So, in this same church women are speaking! They are not sitting down and being silent. They are not quiet! Let's make it make sense. Let's go back to First Corinthians chapter 14, but go up a few verses to 28, "But if there be no interpreter, let him keep silence in the church; and let him speak to himself, and to God." There was chaos in this church. Lots of confusion was taking place. Apostle Paul just shut some men up who were disrupting the service by speaking in tongues. Then as you read down Paul is setting the house in order. Back to verse 34 and 35. Let your women keep silence. "Your." Wait... Paul just addressed women prophesying and praying. What's going on here? It's an easy answer. Verse 35 says let them learn by asking their husbands. These men's wives were new Christians and the husbands knew enough to teach them at home. Their wives were disrupting church services. Look at this entire chapter. Apostle Paul is setting things in order, and please remember chapter 11 where women were prophesying and praying. Women, if you're in a church teaching you to shut up, leave. Women, if you're at a church and you can't speak, leave. Women, if you know you're called to ministry and you're shut down from doing anything in your church, leave. This is bondage and control.

Now let's talk about what Apostle Paul said in the book of Timothy. First Timothy chapter 1 verses 1 & 2, "Paul, an apostle of Jesus Christ by the commandment of God our Savior, and Lord Jesus Christ, which is our hope; Unto Timothy, my own son in the faith: Grace, mercy, and peace, from God our Father and Jesus Christ our Lord." This epistle is written to Timothy. It's not addressed to any church. This epistle is not to the body of Christ. This letter is to Timothy. Look at First Corinthians chapter 1 verse 2, "Unto the church of God which is at Corinth." Paul's letter to Corinth was addressed to the entire church. Paul says to Timothy, "Let no man despise thy youth; but be thou an example of the believers, in word, in conversation, in charity (love), in spirit, in faith, in purity. First Timothy chapter 4 verse 12. Apostle Paul was probably responding to an epistle Timothy wrote him. First Timothy chapter 4 verse 13 says, "Till I come, give attention to reading, to exhortation, to doctrine." Timothy was a young pastor. Let no man despise your youth is Paul telling Timothy to have some backbone and walk in his authority against his haters until he comes to set his church in order. Well, during my years as a Christian, I have witnessed women trying to usurp authority. It happened to me. I talked about her on page 74 in this book. Usurp is a very strong thing to do in the church. Usurp: to seize and hold by force or without legal authority.

To take over or occupy without right:

To take the place of without legal authority; supplant.

To seize another's place, authority, or possession wrongfully.

I personally believe Timothy was the pastor of a small church that had a bunch of women who were also older than him. Remember this epistle is written to Timothy and not to a church. Yet, you have so many churches today teaching from the Timothy books as if these words were addressed to the church. Timothy's church had many women who were Christians who knew much more than him. The issue was they didn't respect him as pastor and tried to take over. No one in this church were mature Christians. Maturity in Christ wouldn't try to usurp God's ordained authority in God's church. Moreover, maturity in Christ would understand God uses women in ministry. I said what I said, and I'm not apologizing. There is neither male or female in Christ. Ladies seek the Lord if you're in a church holding you hostage with those verses we just went over. Be free in the name of Jesus. You are accountable to God first; not your pastor. Write a letter resigning from your church and move on in Christ. If the church leadership is speaking curses against your life and ministry, I break them in the name of Jesus. I loose the blessings of Christ over your life and your ministry in the name of Jesus. I bind every spirit of retaliation against my life, my books, my family, my ministry, my business, and all that Christ has called me to do in the mighty matchless name of Jesus. Be free in the name of Jesus. Amen. Like I said earlier, you cannot take a verse of scripture and build a doctrine or message that doesn't line up with other verses of scripture in the bible. Clearly these verses we just went over do not line up together. Women of God be free in the liberty Christ has given us all in the body of Christ. Fulfill your ministry in the peace which passes all understanding the Lord gives us in the name of Jesus.

Now let's talk about church leadership against other church leadership. Once again maturity in Christ would have the love of Christ and the grace of God when you address all issues. Here's what I wrote in my book, "WHAT TO DO WHEN YOU KNOW YOUR PASTOR IS WRONG."

"A pastor speaking evil against another pastor is another issue that occurs quite often. Whether on television, on conference platforms, or on radio, these things ought not to be. Some even establish websites and blogs to try to prove another pastor is wrong or false. I've heard of many attacks on social media. I'm not a pastor, but I experienced such an attack on social media. A minister and I had a doctrinal disagreement. This minister started attacking me on social media. I boldly told him he was wrong and he went all out trying to destroy me on social media. Even though his attack was brutal, everyone witnessed how the Lord moved on my behalf and revealed just how wrong this minister was openly. I felt bad for him cause his attack on me ended up destroying his ministry. He soon deleted his social media pages and has not been seen on social media since. None of us as Christians should be attacking each other on any platform. These things should not be people of God. Especially when it comes to pastors against other pastors.

When you are wrong about the pastor, you're criticizing you're fighting the work of God. Now you're an enemy to the work of God. This is a great evil. Criticizing pastors when you do not have any idea of what the Lord told them to do. In Mark chapter 10 verses 38 and 39 reads, "And John answered him, saying, Master, we saw one casting out devils in thy name, and he followeth not us: and we forbad him, because he followeth not us. But Jesus said, Forbid him not: for there is no man which shall do a miracle in my name, that can lightly speak evil of me." In these scriptures Jesus told his disciples not to stop the one doing miracles in his name although he didn't follow them. In other words, this person (pastor) did not receive the training, the instructions, and the insight from Jesus hands on, but Jesus said forbid him not. Just because another pastor doesn't do it how you were taught does not make them wrong in what they are doing for Jesus. Although this person (pastor) did not personally receive what the disciples received hands on from Jesus, this person (pastor) still operated in the power of Jesus. Now if Jesus said forbid him not, why are you criticizing another pastor's ministry because it's not like your own? Leave another man's work alone and work on your own ministry. As Christians we fight against spirits of darkness and we contend with our own flesh. Why must we attack each other? Yes there are false doctrines and false Christian churches, but Jesus said my sheep know my voice and a stranger they will not follow. The only people who will follow a false prophet, false pastor, or false doctrine, are the people that do not have their names are not written in the Lambs book of Life. You don't have to attack that pastor on your platform, on television, on radio, or on the internet. Pray and ask the Lord to save everyone who's operating in false doctrine. It's bad enough that those operating in false doctrine, and spirits of error, are on their way to hell. Let's pray for God to show them mercy and enlighten them to the truth. Maybe some will be saved. However, if you are speaking evil against a pastor who's sent by God, you're now fighting against God Himself. Remember pastors reap what they sow too. Someone just might believe that you are teaching false doctrine one day, and do to you what you did to another pastor. Remember Matthew chapter 7 verse 2, "For with what judgment ye judge, ye shall be judged: and with what measure ye mete, it shall be measured to you again." God has no respect of persons. We all reap what we sow in the House of God and abroad. Even the non-Christians reap what they sow. They tend to say, "What goes around, comes around." In actuality this is the same principle. What you do to others will befall yourself. Of course, we all understand what happened when Jesus came on the scene. The Pharisees and Sadducees did not receive his doctrine. Jesus also said that the traditions of men have caused the word of God to be of no effect. Jesus did not follow their traditions and Jesus did only what His Father told him to do. This is the same exact thing that is happening today. The traditional church pastors are attacking the nontraditional church pastors who are not following the religious traditions. In the book of Acts chapter 5 verse 29 KJV says, "Then Peter and the other apostles answered and said, We ought to obey God rather than men."

Just because another pastor isn't doing what you're doing doesn't make that pastor wrong. After they were filled with the Holy Ghost the apostles went through many hard situations with the Pharisees and Sadducees because they did not follow their religious traditions. Even the churches today, which are not walking in religious tradition, are criticized and talked about negatively by the traditional churches. In the same chapter of the book of Acts verses 34 through 39 reads, "Then stood there up one in the council, a Pharisee, named Ga-ma'-li-el, a doctor of the law, had in reputation among all the people, and commanded to put the apostles forth a little space; And said unto them, Ye men of Israel, take heed to yourselves what ye intend to do as touching these men. For before these days rose up Theu'-das, boasting himself to be somebody; to whom a number of men, about four hundred, joined themselves: who was slain; and all, as many as obeyed him, were scattered, and brought to nought. After this man rose up Judas of Galilee in the days of the taxing, and drew away much people after him: he also perished; and all, even as many as obeyed him, were dispersed. And now I say unto you, Refrain from these men, and let them alone: for if this counsel or this work be of men, it will come to nought: But if it be of God, ye cannot overthrow it; lest haply ye be found even to fight against God." If any pastor or church is not of God it will come to nothing. You don't have to criticize these pastors or talk evil about these pastors. However, if you are speaking evil of a pastor who is sent and anointed by God, now you are fighting against God and touching God's anointed. Take heed to Gamaliel and not touch the pastors who you believe are wrong or false. If their work is not of God it will eventually come to nothing.

If your pastor is speaking evil of another pastor, pray diligently for your pastor. If you see a pastor on any platform speaking evil of another pastor pray for that pastor as well. Many fellow Christians are enemies to God's work unconsciously and indirectly, even as Saul (Paul) thought he was doing a work for God by laying waste the Christians. In Acts chapter 8 verse 3 Amplified Bible says, "But Saul shamefully treated and laid waste the church continuously [with cruelty and violence]; and entering house after house, he dragged out men and women and committed them to prison." In Acts chapter 9 verse 4 Amplified Bible, the Lord Himself tells Saul, "Saul, Saul, why are you persecuting Me [harassing, troubling, and molesting Me]?" Saul was a Pharisee and held fast to their religious traditions. Saul thought he was doing God a favor by persecuting the Christians, but it turned out that Saul was persecuting God Himself. After Saul was converted, and his name was changed to Paul, he wrote this in Philippians chapter 1 verse 15 through 18 KJV, "Some indeed preach Christ even of envy and strife; and some also of good will: The one preach Christ of contention, not sincerely, supposing to add affliction to my bonds: But the other of love, knowing that I am set for the defense of the gospel. What then? Notwithstanding, every way, whether in pretence, or in truth, Christ is preached; and I therein do rejoice, yea, and will rejoice." There you have it from the mouth of Paul. As long as Christ is being preached be happy. Now I'm talking about pastors who are in the churches who believe Jesus is the son of God and the only way to the Father. Pastors who teach from Genesis to Revelation. Pastors who are standing on all of the word of God. Now that I made that clear let's continue. You may not believe in what they are doing, but so what if you don't agree with their methodology. It doesn't mean it's not God's work because you don't have their revelation. Every pastor has a different vision from the Lord and a different assignment. Every pastor will carry out their vision and assignment by whatever means the Lord instructs. Please don't find yourself persecuting God's work and the Lord's anointed." Paragraph 1 page 100. Please stop coming against other pastors. Luke chapter 9 verses 49 and 50, "And John answered and said, Master, we saw one casting out devils in thy name; and we forbade him, because he followeth not us. And Jesus said unto him, Forbid him not: for he that is not against us is for us." Here's a good example. Jesus said leave them alone. They weren't trained like you. They didn't grow up in the church like you. They didn't attend bible college like you. Their church has a different order than yours. Whatever your reason for coming against them, please stop it. If you really believe they are wrong, pray on their behalf or intercede for their church. Adding negative attention to the body of Christ is not going to make you look like a good Christian. If only we really loved each other how Christ commanded, the body of Christ would be so much better.

What I am about to talk about last is the thing I've experienced in every church I've been a member of. I experienced this with multiple pastors who will not be named and I will not describe them or say anything that will describe their churches. If you know me personally, or corporately, because we were members of the same church, please do not disclose the identities of these pastors or their churches. This book is not to attack anyone. God told me to write this book. This book was nowhere in my mind until God spoke to me as I took a shower. Let's start off with James chapter 3 verses 13 through 18, "Who is a wise man and endued with knowledge among you? Let him show out of a good conversation his works with meekness of wisdom. But if ye have bitter envying and strife in your hearts, glory not, and lie not against the truth. This wisdom descendeth not from above, but is earthly, sensual, devilish. For where envying and strife is, there is confusion and every evil work. But the wisdom that is from above is first pure, then peaceable, gentle, and easy to be entreated, full of mercy and good fruits, without partiality, and without hypocrisy. And the fruit of righteousness is sown in peace of them that make peace."

Partiality: 1. Prejudice or bias in favor of something.

2. A special fondness: a predilection:

Predilection: A special liking for something; a preference.

>   A predisposition, preference, or bias
>   A tendency to think favorably of
>   something in particular; partiality;
>   preference.
> Peace: The absence of war or other hostilities.
>   Freedom from quarrels and disagreement.
>   Public security and order.
>   In a state of tranquility; serene.
>   Free from strife.
>   To be silent.
>   A state of harmony between people or groups;
>   A state of stillness, silence, or serenity
>   To bring hostilities to an end.

I believe these verses of scripture will cover most of everything associated with what I am about to talk about in church leadership. Every church I've been a member of are guilty of "Respect Of Persons." I'm guilty of respect of persons and when God rebuked me I repented. I'll share exactly what I did momentarily when I was in the inner circle. I learned some bad behavior and I'm glad God rebuked me for it. Much of my learned inner circle behavior I needed to be delivered and purged of by God. God does not have respect of persons. There are verses in the bible in the Old and New Testament on respect of persons. God hates respect of persons. Let's see how much God hates it.

Leviticus chapter 19 verse 15, "Ye shall do no unrighteousness in judgment: thou shalt not respect the person of the poor, nor honor the person of the mighty: but in righteousness shalt thou judge thy neighbor."

Deuteronomy chapter 1 verse 17, "Ye shall not respect persons in judgment; but ye shall hear the small as well as the great; ye shall not be afraid of the face of man; for the judgment is God's: and the cause that is too hard for you, bring it unto me, and I will hear it."

Deuteronomy chapter 16 verse 19 "Thou shalt not wrest judgement thou shalt not respect persons, neither take a gift: for a gift doth blind the eyes of the wise, and pervert the words of the righteous."

Second Chronicles chapter 19 verse 7, "Wherefore now let the fear of the LORD be upon you; take heed and do it: for there is no iniquity with the LORD our God, nor respect of person, nor taking of gifts."

Proverbs chapter 24 verse 23, "These things also belong to the wise. It is not good to have respect of persons in judgment."

Proverbs chapter 28 verse 21, "To have respect of persons is not good: for a piece of bread that man will transgress."

Acts chapter 10 verse 34, "Then Peter opened his mouth, and said, Of a truth I perceive that God is no respecter of persons."

Romans chapter 2 verse 11, "For there is no respect of persons with God."

Ephesians chapter 6 verse 9, "And, ye masters, do the same things unto them, forbearing threatening: knowing that your Master also is in heaven; neither is there respect of persons with him."

Colossians chapter 3 verse 25, "But he that doeth wrong shall receive for the wrong which he hath done: and there is no respect of persons."

First Peter chapter 1 verse 17, "And if ye call on the Father, who without respect of persons judgeth according to every man's work, pass the time of your sojourning here in fear."

Well, that was a lot, but wait, there's more. I'll continue with another verse on respect of persons in a moment. The world hates being judged. "You can't judge me etc.." However, there are plenty of verses on judging situations. "Do ye not know that the saints shall judge the world? and if the world shall be judged by you, are ye unworthy to judge the smallest matters? Know ye not that we shall judge angels? How much more things that pertain to this life? If then ye have judgments of things pertaining to this life, set them to judge who are least esteemed in the church." First Corinthians chapter 6 verses 2 through 4. We are the saints of God and Apostle Paul says "We" shall judge the world, and "We" shall judge angels. Think of everyone you ever shared Christ with and the people you talked to about salvation. We are going to judge them. I know this is so deep if not too deep for many of you reading this right now. Let's continue.

Let's talk about the instructions Apostle Paul gave

the church at Corinth. He said, "set them to judge who are least esteemed in the church." Think of church issues that we commonly have today. Think of the people in your church who are least esteemed or least recognized in your church. Apostle Paul told them to let the people at the bottom of the bottom in the church judge the situation. How many churches do this today? Well, I haven't been to every church across the globe, but I can safely say the church leadership will be called upon to handle every situation. Just think of what Apostle Paul instructed. The least person should be the judge. Not the pastor, not the prophet, not the apostle, or anyone in church leadership. He said the least esteemed. Who would that be in your church? Now the person who just entered your mind, who is this person? Write it down why they are the least esteemed and ask yourself, "Do you have the love of Christ or the grace of God toward this person?" Probably not huh? Who is the least person in your church? Judge your heart right now. How do you feel about this person, or persons? How would you feel having this person judge your situation? How would you feel having this person counsel you? Be honest right now. If your heart isn't filled with the love of Christ and / or the grace of God towards them at this very moment, you have respect of persons. Even as I type these words I can feel so much conviction that's going to take place. Would you let this person counsel you or judge your situation? Could you? If yes, amen. If not..., why? Why wouldn't you? God is exposing heart conditions right now. Seek the Lord about it church leadership.

Are you the person who's least esteemed in your church? Are you the person on the bottom? I know how that feels. That's what my first book is about. I was elevated to church leadership and then I wrongfully became the least esteemed in our church, but God brought through it. Maybe I was tied with being the least esteemed with a few other individuals, but I know what that feels like to be at the bottom within a church. Maybe some people never considered who the least person may be in their church. Now here's the next verse on respect of persons.

James chapter 2 verses 1 through 9, "My brethren, have not the faith of our Lord Jesus Christ, the Lord of glory, with respect of persons. For if there come unto your assembly a man with a gold ring, in goodly apparel, and there come in also a poor man in vile raiment; And ye have respect to him that weareth the gay clothing, and say unto him, Sit thou here in a good place; and say to the poor, Stand thou there, or sit here under my footstool: Are ye not then partial in yourselves, and are become judges of evil thoughts? Hearken, my beloved brethren, Hath not God chosen the poor of this world rich in faith, and heirs of the kingdom which he hath promised to them that love him? But ye have despised the poor. Do not rich men oppress you, and draw you before the judgment seats? Do not they blaspheme that worthy name by the which ye are called? If ye fulfil the royal law according to the scripture, Thou shalt love they neighbor as thyself, ye do well: But if ye have respect to persons, ye commit sin, and are convinced of the law as transgressors."

Hey ushers, how are you doing? Respect of persons is called sin and these verses point out the guilty parties as judges of evil thoughts. I've seen this before when homeless people enter the church. I visited a certain church on a certain night and there was a homeless man who had a smell I recognized. He was the guy who rode my train when I worked at the Chicago Transit Authority. "There was this one man who rode the train who had maggots on him. It was one of the worst smells I've ever breathed. One night I visited a church and when I walked inside, there was that same smell. That same man was sitting in this church and no one sat anywhere near him. I don't know what his health issues were, but he rode our trains regularly. He always had a newspaper and placed it in his seat before he sat down. I called him "The Newspaper Man."" From my book, "I LOVED WORKING AT THE CTA. The Memoirs Of A Public Transit Train Operator In Chicago." I didn't go any further about what happened at this church. This man was in the rear of this church and no one sat within 10 rows of him. I was a customer assistant one night instead of being on the train. This man walked into my station and stood in the distance. On this night he looked good. He had a haircut and clean clothes. I approached him and said, "I saw you at (such and such) church. Did anyone help you or give you money?" No one helped him. He went to a shelter that allowed him to bathe and gave him some fresh clothing. They also gave him a haircut. This church has a big name in Chicago. He smelled terrible, but where was the love of Christ that night? I'm sure this church had plenty of resources to assist this homeless man. Respect of persons was the issue. He waited for someone to approach him after church and no one came near him or spoke to him. No one even came to tell him to leave when the church was empty. Who was the person to make sure the church is empty? Wow! They waited until this homeless man exited their church and never said a word to him.

Respect of persons covers many things and remember, it's sin. I'm about to share things pastors have done to me personally that was respect of persons. Some of these things will be simple things and other things will be serious. There was a pastor who I wrote a letter to because there was a matter I wanted them to look into. I later asked this pastor if they read my letter and they confirmed they read it. Well, they never responded to me concerning my letter. Not a yes or no. Not a meeting or appointment was established to talk. My matter was ignored. I'm so happy Christ will never ignore me. Every matter of my heart is important and handled by Christ. Christ will never put my matters on the backburner, ignore me, or forget about me.

The incident I talked about earlier in this book about the woman who had a Jezebel spirit, well, our pastor took her side in the situation. Like I said I was openly rebuked. There was also a meeting about the situation and I was further rebuked openly. When I say I felt so low afterwards. When I returned to our church for the next service, I wasn't even comfortable anymore. I continued attending until my pastor and I had a conversation after church a few weeks later. I was very transparent that I no longer felt comfortable in our church anymore. My pastor responded, "If you don't feel comfortable here anymore, maybe you should find another church where you will be comfortable." Wow! There was no love of Christ or the grace of God in these words. I felt as if my pastor was kicking me out of our church. Where were the words, "Well, give it some time. We need to pray through this season and look to God..." I couldn't believe my ears. After the meeting we had a few weeks earlier, many people left the church because of other issues that happened along with my situation. There was a big mess of things taking place all at the same time and our meeting talked about each one. I wasn't the only person rebuked that day and I didn't believe rebuke was the way to go. I endured my rebuke even though I believed it wasn't justified. In my case the pastor had respect of persons toward the woman who wanted my position. Why couldn't he rebuke her by saying, "Brother Marcus is the leader of (blah) and you are to listen to him." It was simple. I ended up resigning, feeling unwanted, and believing my own pastor held the door open for me to exit. You know how someone looks as they hold the door open for you? This is exactly how I felt. Why stay at a church when my own pastor wants me to leave? I later heard most of the church members resigned as well. More than half to be exact. I prayed about this until I heard from God. My pastor didn't handle this situation correctly. However, God does have grace toward ministry assignments He has ordained. What do I mean? Let me explain. If you're a pastor who keeps doing something that causes people to leave your church, God shows you grace by sending more people to your church. The grace of God is sending you more people. The grace of God is keeping your church open. The grace of God keeps sending your church new souls to fulfil the purpose God has called you to do in ministry. If your church is a revolving door of people who come and go, come and go, and come and go, pastor you need to examine yourself in the faith. Ask God why this keeps happening. Seek the Lord. Ask God to let you see yourself pastor and see your church leadership through God's eyes. You need to find out the root of the real issue that you have with

God's people. It's clearly respect of persons, but chances are you're full of pride, arrogant, and living in denial that you're the problem. You have to know how to treat God's people with the love of Christ and respect of persons in your heart will not allow the love of Christ. Let's reiterate James chapter 3 verses 13 through 18 again. The emphasis is on 13 through 16. Verse 13; are your conversations full of meekness of wisdom pastor? Verse 14; do you have strife and envy in your heart pastor? Verse 16; is your church leadership or church congregation; or both, full of envying, full of strife, and full of confusion? Be honest now. There's always some crazy situation you have to deal with concerning your members. Is there confusion and strife among the church leadership? Do you have every evil work in your church pastor? I've seen church leadership cover up everything from the congregation, but all of the church leadership know the truth about everything. Verse 17; this is the wisdom you should possess. It's first pure, peaceable, gentle, and easy to be entreated. I've seen pastors and church leadership react with nasty attitudes many times over. No shade thrown, but I've seen it many times. Where is peace in your church? Remember the fruit of righteousness is sown in peace of them that make peace. Where are the peacemakers in your church? "Blessed are the peacemakers: for they shall be called the children of God." Matthew chapter 5 verse 9. If there are no peacemakers in your church, are y'all the children of God? Where is the love of Christ? Where are the people sowing peace in your church? Peace is a fruit of the Holy Spirit. The pastor and church leadership should be full of mercy, good fruits (the fruit of the Spirit Galatians chapter 5 verses 22 & 23 love, joy, peace, patience, gentleness, goodness, faith, meekness, and temperance.), and without partiality or hypocrisy. We already read the definition of partiality. Here's hypocrisy.

Hypocrisy: The practice of professing beliefs, feelings, or virtues that one does not hold or possess; falseness.

An act or instance of such falseness.

It's really sad if you're a hypocrite in church leadership. You should have been proven prior to your elevation or ordination. If you're a fake shame on you. It's hard to fake love, kindness, mercy, the love of Christ, and the grace of God. The fruit of the Spirit are developed in the presence of God. You can try to be fake, but faking it won't last. At some point the fake covers will be removed. One day you'll have the right combination of circumstances that will trigger the real you. We must all have the genuine fruit of the Holy Ghost. Church leadership must continue to seek the Lord and spend time in the presence of God. If you're not seeking God, or spending time with God, you are in the flesh. You are a carnal Christian. Study the book of Romans.

"Pastors have to remember that the members of their church are not just their members, but also God's sons and daughters. Pastors must be good stewards over God's people. Many people attend church without walking in an office or have a title in front of their name. No matter who you are in the church, all of us, especially pastors, must be careful how we treat God's children. That person without the position and title just might be anointed by the Lord. They may just be a bench member for now, but that doesn't mean they are not anointed. There are many gifts in the body of Christ and there are many unknown anointed Christians. There are more unknown anointed Christians than popular anointed Christians. They seek the Lord in secret and God has anointed them in secret. Soon their gifts will make room for them in the body of Christ. Touch not my anointed goes for pastors as well. Pastors must always keep in mind that they will give an account for their flock one day. It's best for them to be conscious of this very thing every day. Because pastors will give an account for each person in their church they should go before the Lord in prayer before they handle any situation with the members of their church." From my book, "WHAT TO DO WHEN YOU KNOW YOUR PASTOR IS WRONG" paragraph 1 page 15.

Pastors should be the example of the love of Christ and the grace of God. The church leadership should follow their pastor's example. Then the congregation follows all of you. "Be ye followers of me, even as I also am of Christ." First Corinthians chapter 11 verse 1. Apostle Paul said follow him as he follows Christ. This is the example for all church leadership. If you're not mature enough to be in church leadership please resign. You're going to give an account for how you treat God's people. Partiality and hypocrisy in church leadership is a terrible thing. Stop having respect of persons. Get it together before the Lord's hand is released against you like the churches in the book of Revelation.

When church leadership has respect of persons,

partiality takes place in various ways. Here's a real life example. A man and woman were married. The husband was in church leadership and the wife was not a church leader. The husband was respected among the church leadership and the congregation. This same husband who prays before the church, who counsels, and does many other things cheated on his wife. Then he cheated on his wife again. The wife decided to get counseling from someone in the church leadership of the same church. This person in church leadership identified one of the situations the wife brought to their attention. The wife was told what their husband did was nothing. I cannot give all of the details. Just know the husband achieved an orgasm from a woman that was not his wife. This person in church leadership had respect of persons. This wasn't just poor counseling. Everyone should know this is sin and adultery. How can you say this is nothing? The wife decided to file for divorce. She stayed at the same church and her husband remained in church leadership. Her husband started lying on her saying that she cheated and that's why their marriage is over. She never cheated, but guess what? The church leadership believed her husband. She was alienated in their church. She was shunned and talked about as if she was a whore. When she talked to me about her situation, I encouraged her in the Lord. She endured this situation with the help of the grace of God. Here's the hard truth about this situation. Where was the ear to hear from God? How come no one asked or sought God about this situation? This is a very sad situation for this church who is supposed to be full of discernment and the Spirit of God. Often times God shows me when people are lying. So no one in this church leadership discerned her husband was lying? So, God didn't speak to no one? Shaking my head. To make matters worse, the church leadership spread his lies about his wife. Does this sound like any verses we went over in this book? Of course. Let's add another. "Lie not one to another, seeing that ye have put off the old man with his deeds;" Colossians chapter 3 verse 9. Here's what this husband in church leadership should have done. "Can you keep us in prayer? We are getting a divorce." No lies were needed to say this. All of you liars are going to reap what you sowed. Why does church leadership act as if God is not watching? Depart from me is a real thing. This couple is now divorced and this lie is still believed. No one came to her to hear her side. She was pushed away. Where is the love of Christ? This is respect of persons. They showed respect to their fellow church leader and didn't have any respect for his wife. They heard him and had a closed ear to hear her. This is respect of persons. How can you make a judgment without hearing both sides? Can you imagine a courtroom where only one side is heard and the jury makes a decision?

Here's another form of respect of persons. You're called to ministry, but no one gives you a chance to go forth with your ministry. However, they allow others to go forth with their ministry. You hear things to keep you from going forth in ministry. This is to purposely discourage you. Meanwhile, you'll see others around you being encouraged to go forth in ministry. This is respect of persons.

Because you're rejected through respect of persons, God encourages you to start your ministry outside of your church. When your church leadership hears about it, they want you to shut it down and stop it altogether, or they simply tell everyone not to support you. This is respect of persons. I've heard pastors tell people to stop their ministry outside of their church and say that's not God leading you, but they never let them go forth in ministry within their church. I know many Christians who resigned from their church because of respect of persons, and now they are going forth in ministry freely. I know others who sat down in their church 10 plus years before they decided to resign from their church. The pastor kept saying they were going to let them go forth in ministry, but never allowed them to do so. God shifted them to another place to be free to go forth in ministry. This is respect of persons.

Please seek the Lord and let Him guide you where you need to be to go forth in ministry when it's your time. Do not sit in a church where the pastor and the church leadership is keeping you from going forth in ministry. I'm not talking to new Christians. I'm talking to those who have several years under their belt and who are mature enough to handle ministry.

Respect of person also goes outside of ministry and the church walls. Respect of person shows its ugly head in many other ways. You start a business and no one at your church supports it; not even your pastor. You wrote a book and no one at your church supports it. They don't even acknowledge it. It's so sad. When these things happen we call it many other things such as rejection, envy, jealously, and they are some haters. It's respect of persons. Then you witness others start a business and get support from the church. You see others write a book and everyone buys it. This is book number 18 and I know people who have never bought 1 of my books, but I witnessed them buying books from others in our church. I kept it before the Lord so I wouldn't be bitter, angry, or upset. I thank God for those who do support me. Let God's will be done. Amen.

Respect of persons in judgement comes when your pastor, or church leadership counselor, always side with the person accusing you or saying you did a certain thing. It's very clear when you do not have the chance to explain your actions. This is respect of persons. It could be marriage counseling when the counselor always takes the husband's side or always takes the wife's side. It could be an issue between family members and the counselor always takes a certain person's side. It's very sad people of God. Here's another example. You say, "God has given me a word for our church." Yet, you're not allowed to release it to the church. This is respect of persons. You have a dream or vision that's rejected as if you don't know God enough yet, or not at all. You may be shunned, ignored, or talked to in such a way saying you're not ready yet. If you do not feel they are ready to release this word before the church, why not have them tell you the word they received and judge the word to see if it's from God. How can someone grow within a church ministry setting if they are never given the opportunity? Figure it out church leadership.

In a few churches, I witnessed respect of persons toward people who gave the most money to our church. These people's sins and actions were overlooked because they gave plenty of money. I've seen it many times. No matter what issue is brought up against these people with money, the pastor and church leadership sided with the big money givers every time. Why is it some people can never do any wrong? Respect of persons. No matter how they act they are never corrected, rebuked, or sat down from their ministry duties because of respect of persons.

Respect of persons also entails being talked down to as if you're beneath the person you're talking to in church leadership. They talk to you as if you don't know God, or as if you're nowhere near their level of knowledge of Christ. I'm so grateful God doesn't have respect of persons. There are times in Christ where you may seem like Joseph in the book of Genesis who was rejected by his brothers. Rejection hurts, but respect of persons hurts more. It's a deeper form of rejection. Respect of persons can be kindly executed. It can be performed with a smile, but it's still wrong and it still hurts. Church leadership you need to get it together before Christ visits you.

Respect of persons turned me off with ministry inside the church. I pray I never have respect of persons in my character ever again. Here's what I did in church leadership and God rebuked me. Well, I was married and no longer single. There was a single woman of God who was guilty of sexual sin and I didn't show her the grace of God. I had an arrogant attitude as if I was never guilty of sexual sin. I'm so happy the Holy Ghost corrected me and reminded me of my sexual sins. My "FROM WOMAN TO WOMAN" tell-all books contain all of my sexual sins. 18+ readers only. Extremely transparent. Adult language and strong sexual themes. These books are not for you religious and self-righteous Christians. I'll never have respect of persons ever again. That's the only time I did this, but guess what? That same woman of God ended up marrying the guy, and they are happily married. I hear they are going forth in ministry together, and my marriage ended in divorce. Never judge a book by its cover. Always have the love of Christ and the grace of God.

Your respected name in ministry doesn't mean anything to Christ if you're operating in respect of persons. It's sin people of God. Church leadership it's sin. It's not adultery or homosexuality, but it's sin. Most pastors have respected names and this is why people give them the benefit of the doubt when they are accused, but guess what? Pastors lie to cover up their sin. They want to keep their respected name. "It's a beautiful thing to see a pastor say I apologize, or I am wrong, in front of the entire church. It's not a bad thing to apologize; it's a good thing to apologize. It's comforting to see a pastor acknowledge a transgression. Pastors make mistakes. Pastors are fallible. A pastor can fall into sin and commit sin just like any of us. Stop looking at your pastor as if he/she does not have any problems, faults, weaknesses, sins, and have it all together. If you study the word of God you will notice that God called plenty of people who had many problems and many weaknesses. We all have weaknesses. Yes, your pastor has weaknesses. Your pastor is not perfect. Do not be surprised if your pastor makes a mistake. Don't be shocked. All have sinned and come short of the glory of God. I pray the mistake is not something criminal. God will still love the pastor and God will forgive the pastor even in his criminal sin. However, if you do the crime you will be doing some time in prison. God says do not suffer as an evil doer." From my book, "WHAT TO DO WHEN YOU KNOW YOUR PASTOR IS WRONG." Line 2 page 99.

Pastors can commit sin like anyone one of us. They are not superhumans. Apostle Paul was given a thorn so everyone would know he's a human being. He's my example. I don't care how great your name is in the earth. You're not above sin and even though you may be heavily anointed by God, you are not the anointing. The anointing in your life is God. It's not you. With that same powerful anointing of God in your life, Christ can still say, "Depart from me your work was in iniquity." People of God always remember you are not the anointing. The anointing in your life should cause you to be a very humble loving Christian. I honor the people of God and will not disrespect any ministry gift God has established. If you commit sin, I'm the person you want to call. As a matter of fact, lots of church leaders call me when they mess up. Why? I'm team Galatians chapter 6 verse 1. I've sinned many times and did not receive the grace of God from the people of God. I received the opposite from self-righteous arrogant church leaders who act as if they have never sinned ever in their life. The stronger your pastor and church leadership appears, the more humble they should be. The more they should be filled with the love of Christ and the grace of God. I don't care how respected their name is in the body of Christ. Christ is the name that is above every name in the church. I respect church leaders, but I know Christ is above you and when you treat me wrong I can go to Him about you. To you new Christians, God does not have respect of persons. If your pastor is wrong, God will rebuke and correct your pastor. Church leadership is under the word of God just like us. They are not above God's word. We are all the servants of God in the body of Christ, and God will judge us all one day. Only the pure at heart shall see God.

Here's another example of respect of persons by a pastor. This church went through a hard season and the finances weren't coming in like they used to. There are many reasons how this can happen. Lots of people leave your church with their money or maybe the people at your church lost their jobs. Maybe the business owners lost their contracts or their business doesn't have finances coming in anymore. I've seen this happen at several churches. Have you ever heard this announcement? "If you can. Can you please give a little more today?" This can be said in many ways. I've always hated when these type of announcements are said with anger or frustration. Even worse than this is when they add, "God said to give..." I'm not talking about sowing a seed. I'm talking about the regular offering. Not giving something extra because you desire to bless the speaker, or the person who released a word of knowledge, or a prophetic word of the Lord in your life. Now here's what happened with this particular church. Well, when the finances started slowing down the church leaders who were on the church payroll, without written notice or verbal notification, receive a check that was greatly reduced from their regular salary. Can you imagine how they felt? They were shocked and started making calls to their pastor. Most of them were greeted by voicemail. After many of them made calls to find out what was going on, they finally got some answers. This particular church couldn't afford to pay the people on their staff anymore. An advanced announcement would have been nice so they could have been prepared. As a matter of fact, why not provide an announcement far in advanced so they could start looking for other streams of income. However, this pastor did not do this. They were quiet. No, they were silent. The church finance department was silent. How do you not inform people they will not receive their regular paycheck? The church leadership on payroll was greatly discouraged when their money wasn't right. This sent all of them in financial crisis and distress. Now this situation revealed a different level of respect of persons. Did the pastor go without any money? This is the question I cannot answer. Could it be that the pastor didn't pay them so they could take care of their own home? Only God knows. Either way this situation is wrong. Like I said earlier, isn't the pastor supposed to be the servant to their congregation? They are the shepherd of the flock and this pastor handled this situation in a very poor manner. Most of this pastor's church leadership resigned and left altogether. This pastor handled this wrong, but the bigger question is this. Why not inform the people laboring in the gospel with you that their checks will be significantly short? Why was this a problem? Do you not value their work? Were they not important to you? I suppose not. I believe it's very clear this is respect of persons. It doesn't make any sense neglecting to inform your church leadership staff they are not going to receive a full paycheck. To make matters worse, this short check they received would also be the last check they received from their church. This church went completely broke. At least this is what was told to the church leadership. Maybe the pastor kept the remaining money for themselves. Only God knows the truth behind this situation. I cannot imagine working a job and this happens. Then I don't receive another check, but I'm still working. What fruit is this? Where is the professionalism? Respect of persons always negates the right thing to do in judgement, in counsel, in church business, in ministry, and with church social functions. Where was the love of Christ in this situation? Would Christ do this? Where was the grace of God in this situation? These church leaders went into a sudden financial crisis. A small check, then no check at all, without a notification from their pastor, or the church financial department. Respect of persons is sin. James chapter 2 verse 9. If you're at a church that has no respect of persons, you have a jewel like the church of Philadelphia in the book of Revelation. This was the only church that didn't need to be corrected by Christ. So if this is the case for the entire body of Christ, then 6 out of 7 churches has issues Christ desires to correct. This is just my opinion on the church numbers, but I've seen respect of persons in every church I've been a member of. I've seen it in churches I've visited and in my friend's churches. Over the years I have received emails and messages on social media about things pastors are guilty of. People desire to hear my opinions. I completely understand why God gave me this book as an assignment.

There is a pastor who shut down a department in their church without informing the people working in that department. They came to church and discovered they were fired without notice. The pastor never informed them. This group of people were very embarrassed finding out they were permanently released of their duties and the kicker is that the other church departments knew about it. This is respect of persons. How can every department in the church have information about the department that was removed, except the people working in the department being removed? It's called respect of persons. This was done on purpose by the pastor. The pastor purposely withheld this decision from the people being removed from church leadership. Like I said earlier, respect of persons always negates the right thing to do in judgement, in counsel, in church business, in ministry, and with church social functions. Where was the love of Christ in this situation? Would Christ do this? Where was the grace of God in this situation? How do you relieve people in your church leadership and do not inform them until they attempt to function during church? I later heard someone asked this pastor, "Why did you do them like that?" The pastor's response was laughter as they walked off. This was bold and proud respect of persons. Those individuals were openly embarrassed and many of them never returned to this church. This situation became hot gossip throughout this church and it spread to those who didn't attend church on this day. Where was the love of Christ? Nowhere to be found in this situation. Everyone who worked in the department that was deleted by the pastor, without notice, were offended by this pastor's actions. Only 1 person from this former department still attends this church. Respect of persons is real. Respect of persons can be very offensive. "But whoso shall offend one off these little ones which believe in me, it were better for him that a millstone were hanged about his neck, and that he were drowned in the depth of the sea. Matthew chapter 18 verse 6. Those least ones in your church are very valuable to

Christ. The same ones Apostle Paul said should be judging situations. You can't treat God's people with respect of persons and think Christ is ok with your actions. Pastors are going to give a serious account.

This will be the last example. I was laying in my bed sleeping when God showed me an image of something else I needed to add to this book. I released the word of the Lord on social media and I added detailed information. Days later I saw one of my former pastors post exactly what I released as the word of the Lord, but they declared it as if God gave it to them. At first I believed God gave them the same word. However, I saw another post by a different pastor that grabbed my attention. As I read this post by the different pastor, I received a word of knowledge which informed me this was my situation. Now the different pastor's post probably had nothing to do with myself, however, I screen shot the post saving it. I deleted their name off of it. As you read this pastor's post, I'm sure you will see why I saved it. Here's the post.

> It will never cease to amaze me how a person that never likes your posts, but then copies it, rewords it a little bit, and claims it as their own! If it came from someone else, give them credit or at least Like their post. It's actually a form of stealing. I know if you post it, then it's fair game, but it still shows a lack of honesty when you just take it without acknowledging the author. I guess some are just more interested in Likes, Views, and Popularity than they are Integrity, Honesty, and Character. Just venting (Haven't done that on FB in awhile!). Had to get that off my chest.

This post made me think of my situation and like I already said, this post was probably not about me. I never considered my post could have been taken which demonstrated I had a pure heart. My post did not get a lot of likes or comments although it did receive a nice amount of love. All of my former pastors never like, comment, or share any of my posts on my social media pages. Now my former pastor who posted the same thing was praised by other church leadership and their followers. One comment said the post was so powerful and added, "You always come up with amazing things from God." Honestly, I knew some of these people who commented. As I thought more about it I realized this post, which you just read, could have been about me. Most pastors have respected names. I can't say my name is respected in like manner. Like I said before, respect of persons will keep people from supporting your ministry, your business, etc., but I can add this as well. Respect of persons will not allow anyone to like, comment, or share your posts. I posted it, but very few liked it and no one shared it. Someone else with a respected name posts it, it's greatly honored, praised, liked, commented, and shared. I gave God the praise nonetheless and didn't get mad about it. God knows the truth. As I wrote this information the Holy Spirit gave me the following verses, "Therefore, behold, I am against the prophets, saith the Lord, that steal my words every one from his neighbor." Jeremiah chapter 23 verse 30. Stealing the word from the Lord that God gave someone else to release is not respected by God. The Lord is against this action. If God didn't give you the word you should not repeat it as if God gave it to you. Like the pastor declared in their post, give the person you got the word of God from credit. Share who posted the word. Share where you heard or received the word of God. Stop declaring "God said" when God didn't say anything to you. When you cannot give someone credit for being the author of the word of the Lord, it's stealing, shows a lack of character, no integrity, and it's not honorable.

Here is something else it shows: respect of persons. You shared the word of the Lord as your own because you do not respect the person who it originated from. If we were all full of the love of Christ, and the grace of God, this would not be an issue. These things would not happen. I'm very sure this happens on a regular basis. For some of you reading this book you are blown away. If you would just seek the Lord and read your bible you will be blown away more often. The bible details so much more than the things we hear in church on a regular basis, and the popular things we hear on social media.

There are plenty of church leadership guilty of taking a word of God someone else declared and made it their own. This is another reason why I loved when I found that Prophet who prophesied the real events to happen in 2020. Anyone who came out saying God showed me 2020, after 2020, does not get any credit. This reminds me of people who have something to say after God has blessed you. "God showed me He was going to do that for you." It's too late! I look at Christians as if they are crazy. When you could have prophesied the word of God you were silent. Now that God have moved you're trying to get some credit now. Get out of here! If you didn't speak it prior to it happening please don't approach me. Why didn't you release the word of God for my life? Why did you keep it to yourself? Was it respect of persons? Could it be you didn't want to release the word of God to me because of how you see my life and walk with Christ? Since you didn't release the word of the Lord to me, were you disobedient to God? Why didn't you release the word of God to me? Why tell me after God performed His word? It's too late! For the new and young Christians who may not understand, here's some information for you.

"Prophecy should build us up, it should establish us, and instruct and improve our well-being in moral and biblical knowledge. Prophecy should encourage us, stir up the gifting of God on the inside of us, and urge us to press on into the Lord and abroad. We should be strengthened after receiving prophecy, we should have hope after receiving prophecy, and we should be consoled from grief and trouble after receiving prophecy. Prophecy should cheer me up and console me from the troubles of life." From my book "Tainted Influence. Identifying Prophetic Truth & Error" Paragraph 1 line 4 page 34. Telling me a prophetic word you had that you didn't release to me, after God already performed it is useless. Why tell me now? Many times God gives us a prophetic word because He desires to encourage us to stand and to endure life while we are waiting on His promises to be fulfilled. Not giving me what God said concerning my life is keeping me from being built up, consoled, cheered up, and receiving strength as I wait on God to do what He said He would do. So, God gave you a word for me and you didn't tell me. I hate hearing church leadership say, "It wasn't time to release the word to you." So, when is the right time to release a word from God? What is the wrong time to release a word? So, God gave you a word for me and now you want to tell me after God has performed it? Please be quiet. I have no respect or honor for you people of God who do this. Please do not come to me afterwards. Since you were quiet, please remain quiet at this point. Saying it now is useless and it will not edify me at all. YoI have a big example of this in my book, "A Pastor's Mistake." My pastor had a word for me and didn't tell me until after the fact. Immediately in that moment I released my anger at my pastor to the point where his armorbearer thought I was going to beat up our pastor.

What bible verse do you use to justify withholding the word of the Lord? Please tell me. Now, what verse do you use to justify telling me the word of the Lord after God has already established it in my life? Please tell me. I'm so glad God is faithful. God is faithful to His children although many people in His church leadership aren't faithful to those in their congregations. It's such a wonderful feeling knowing God doesn't have respect of persons. We are all equal to God. Some of us have greater levels of God's grace depending on the intent of our heart, how humble we are, and if we are seeking God or not. This is the different maker in many ways, but God doesn't have respect of persons. If God gave you a word for me, why would you not tell me?

"Now I want to talk about warring a good warfare because of prophecy. First Timothy chapter 1 verse 18 KJV reads, "This charge I commit unto thee, son Timothy, according to the prophecies which went before on thee, that thou by them mightest war a good warfare;" Prophecy is also used to keep us encouraged in our walk with the Lord. God may have your pastor speak things in your life that are well in your future to help you endure hardness as a good soldier. Plainly speaking: the prophecy you received will help you to stand through tough situations in your life. Those same prophetic words will keep you praying and seeking God while you're going through painful and almost hopeless situations; which is good warfare. When you receive destiny prophetic words you have to hold on to those words. If you have them recorded or on video, put them in a safe place because you're going to have to hear them repeatedly to remind you of what God has for you. So many times in my own walk with the Lord I had to listen to my prophecies repeatedly just to gain strength to keep enduring hard situations. When you receive destiny prophetic words, God will always give you several more prophetic words by different people that repeat what you have already heard. This is to keep you encouraged and focused on what God has for you in the future. It's called a word of confirmation for those who may not have this knowledge. Whenever we receive a word of confirmation God is sending strength, encouragement, and comfort. He is also reminding us that He is with us and that He is going to perform what He said He was going to do. Many times in my own Christian walk I felt like God was nowhere to be found and when I least expected it, here comes a word of confirmation right when I needed to hear it. Talk about tears of relief and tears of joy. It is so soothing to know God is with us especially when we are going through some pressing situations." From my book, "Tainted Influence. Identifying Prophetic Truth & Error." Paragraph 1 page 54.

Respect of persons happens in various ways. I remember when I visited a certain church and I was with my friend who knew the pastor of this church. My friend and I approached this pastor together. I immediately noticed the pastor did not face me at all. Neither did this pastor turn to acknowledge me. This pastor faced my friend the entire time. I was prepared to greet this pastor and say how I enjoyed their church service. You couldn't miss me standing there. There was no one else around the 3 of us. As soon as their conversation ended this pastor walked off without saying anything to me. As this pastor walked off, I instantly remembered this pastor was an associate of someone in church leadership at my own church who operated in respect of persons. Sometimes we will never know why people have respect of persons against us. I didn't know this pastor, but this pastor acted exactly how the person they knew at my church acted. God has given me discernment to clearly see respect of persons. I've never heard anyone in the church identify actions as

respect of persons. Where was the love of Christ? I promise you there are too many church leaders who do not have the love of Christ, but I'm very sure they want to go to heaven. No love no heaven. Your ministry work is in vain if you have no love. I was offended by this pastor, but I gave it to God in prayer. I'll never visit their church again. What happened to common courtesy?
Courtesy: Politeness, kindness, consideration
      Polite behavior. A polite gesture or remark
      Good manners

    I have no clue why this pastor ignored me. Seeds of discord, gossip, and lies exist in the church. It's all sin church leadership. Let me say this. The anointing and the gifts of God in our lives belong to God. We are not the gift and we are not the anointing. Jesus will say one day to some, "Depart from me your work was in iniquity." There were times when being ignored by pastors and church leadership was crushing to me. Now it's ok because I know and understand that's not how God feels about me. I know I didn't do anything to them to deserve this treatment. Now if I did do something, ok, I get it, but when I don't know you at all and you can't even speak to me at your church pastor; wow! You heard something about me and you do not have the grace of God, the love of Christ, or common courtesy to even speak to me. My books are very transparent. When I mess up I admit it! I'm not a self-righteous Christian. Self-righteous Christians think they are better than others because they are not guilty of certain sins. You're not better than me because I was a whoremonger (Ladies Man-Mack Daddy-Player-Pimp) and you were a real virgin when you got married. I'm not better than the lgbtqia community because I've never been with a man sexually. All of these feelings and thoughts are called self-righteousness. Christ died for all sin. Christ didn't just die for the few sins you people who grew up in the church committed. Christ died for all sin including the sins you have never experienced and find absolutely disgusting. You're not better than anyone in the world. Saul, before God changed his name to Apostle Paul, murdered Christians and look how God used him. Paul considered himself the least of all Apostles. Who are you to think you're better than other Christians because they committed deplorable things? You don't receive special treatment from God because you didn't do those things. Luke chapter 7 verse 47 explains that he that was forgiven a little, loves little, and he that is forgiven a lot, loves a lot. Maybe this is why you have respect of persons because you were forgiven a little, so you love a little. I'll stop right here. I could add more situations of respect of persons. I believe you now understand respect of persons in church leadership and like I said earlier, I've seen it in every church. If your church is like the church of Philadelphia, praise God. Please continue in the love of Christ and the grace of God. Do everything Christ has called you to do. Amen.

Pastors and church leadership please humble yourselves. Ask the Lord, "God, am I guilty of respect of persons? Ask God to search your heart and see where you stand on God's scales. Examine yourselves to see if you are in the faith. Second Corinthians chapter 13 verse 5. "Let this mind be in you, which was also in Christ Jesus." Philippians chapter 2 verse 5. Please allow the Lord to change your mind and your thinking toward your brothers and sisters in Christ. Respect of persons will also have the church leadership looking at what a person did sinfully instead of looking at what Jesus did for them with salvation. Respect of persons does not release the grace of God and does not possess the love of Christ. Respect of persons can be very critical of sin in the lives of God's people. It's really sad when someone sins and there is no one to restore their soul in their church. The church leadership will keep someone they do not care for under condemnation with respect of persons. Yet, let someone sin within the church leaderships inner circle and they will pray, restore, and reassure them Christ loves them. I've seen this too. How many Christians are backslidden because of respect of persons? Only God knows.

When new people join your church they do not know God, but they see you. What you do will determine if they stick around to get to know God. Respect of persons causes many Christians to be offended by the actions of church leaders. When I meet backslidden Christians, I talk with them with the love of Christ and I do all I can to restore them in Christ. I try very hard to overcome their anger and rage over being hurt in the church. I've been there and this is why I try to restore their souls in Christ. Just know God didn't hurt you. Please stop blaming God for what the church leadership did to you, and please come back to Jesus. For those of you who's pastor was your spiritual father and his wife was your spiritual mother, if they operated in respect of persons against you, this is a different kind of pain.

The pain of this goes even deeper. In my book "A Pastor's Mistake," my pastor was my spiritual father and I understand how deep the pain travels in your heart. You trusted them completely as if they were your natural father and mother. Here's a word of advice for everyone hurt by church leadership: forgive them. Even if you never get an apology, which you probably won't, forgive them anyway. For a thorough teaching on forgiveness please get my book, "WHAT TO DO WHEN YOU KNOW YOUR PASTOR IS WRONG." Let's all go forward in Christ. Let's seek the Lord and allow Him to purify our hearts, so one day, we hear these words, "Well done, good and faithful servant." Matthew chapter 25 verse 23. Amen. To pastors and everyone in church leadership worldwide, what's in your heart that the enemy has access to use you with respect of persons? If God corrected you of respect of persons, I know you have already repented and cried out to God. Some of you are now seeing yourself within these pages. "The goodness of God leadeth thee to repentance." Romans chapter 2 verse 4. Those of you guilty who still cannot repent, what's in your heart keeping you from repenting? Is it pride? Don't die with those impurities in your heart. The devil uses those things against you. Remember Satan had no place in Jesus and he should have no place in us. Please seek the Lord and ask God to let you see yourself, so you can identify the things in your heart that have you guilty of respect of persons. Don't die operating in respect of persons. To those of you who repented and desire to change, your change is coming. Apologize where needed and continue in Christ. I have no joy exposing anything negative in the body of Christ.

"So that you may prove yourselves to be blameless and guileless, innocent and uncontaminated, children of God without blemish in the midst of a [morally] crooked and [spiritually] perverted generation, among whom you are seen as bright lights [beacons shining out clearly] in the world [of darkness], holding out and offering to everyone the word of life, so that in the day of Christ I will have reason to rejoice greatly because I did not run [my race] in vain nor labor without result."
Philippians chapter 2 verses 15 & 16 amplified bible

Lord I completed your assignment. I bless you and give you glory. May the purpose of this book be fulfilled in the body of Christ throughout the earth. I thank you for using me for your purpose. Hallelujah! To God be the glory both now and forever. Amen.

| About The Author |

Marcus L. Boston is the owner of Unfazed Publishing LLC. He's been a published author since 2007 and shares his entire life in transparency to minister to others. He is a Christian of thirty years (8/23) and has written many books to aid Christians in their walks with Christ. His first book, "A Pastor's Mistake. What To Do When You Know Your Pastor Is Wrong," sparked a lot of controversy and criticism. Marcus was attacked by various Christians thinking he was using real names and exposing people with personal attacks. After these Christians discovered that all names were changed and that the book was written respectfully, he began to get some better reviews.

His trademark in writing is being very transparent. He shares his life in truth in an effort to show non-Christians the grace that God has for himself, is the same grace God has for them. He shares his failures in an effort to help others avoid the same pitfalls he experienced; especially those who didn't grow up in the church. His personal theme is,

"Making The Church A Better Place"

| Book Me |

Would you like to book me for an appearance or speaking engagement? Would you like autographed books? Would you like to become an author with me? Contact me.

mlb@unfazedpublishing.com

224.762.2242 Business Text

Reader Discretion is Advised. Age 18 +

  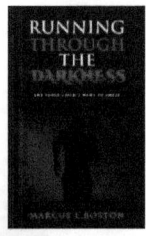 

Available On Amazon - Kindle – IBooks

www.ingramcontent.com/pod-product-compliance
Lightning Source LLC
LaVergne TN
LVHW051051080426
835508LV00019B/1810